SMART SUITS, TATTERED BOOTS

T0324431

Smart Suits, Tattered Boots

*Black Ministers Mobilizing the Black Church
in the Twenty-First Century*

Korie Little Edwards *and* Michelle Oyakawa

NEW YORK UNIVERSITY PRESS
New York

NEW YORK UNIVERSITY PRESS
New York
www.nyupress.org

References to Internet websites (URLs) were accurate at the time of writing. Neither the author nor New York University Press is responsible for URLs that may have expired or changed since the manuscript was prepared.

Library of Congress Cataloging-in-Publication Data
Names: Edwards, Korie L., author. | Oyakawa, Michelle, author.
Title: Smart suits, tattered boots : Black ministers mobilizing the Black church in the twenty-first century / Korie Little Edwards and Michelle Oyakawa.
Description: New York : New York University Press, [2022] | Includes bibliographical references and index.
Identifiers: LCCN 2021013293 | ISBN 9781479808922 (hardback) | ISBN 9781479812530 (paperback : acid-free paper) | ISBN 9781479808946 (ebook) | ISBN 9781479808939 (ebook other)
Subjects: LCSH: African American clergy—Political activity. | Presidents—United States—Election—21st century. | Civil rights movements—United States—History—21st century.
Classification: LCC BR563.N4 E395 2021 | DDC 322/.108996073—dc23
LC record available at https://lccn.loc.gov/2021013293

New York University Press books are printed on acid-free paper, and their binding materials are chosen for strength and durability. We strive to use environmentally responsible suppliers and materials to the greatest extent possible in publishing our books.

Manufactured in the United States of America

10 9 8 7 6 5 4 3 2 1

Also available as an ebook

CONTENTS

The election of 2020 was one for the history books. There were in-person voting lines in which some people stood for six hours to vote and bogus claims of election fraud that went all the way to the Supreme Court, and notably, the president repeatedly declared foul play concerning mail-in ballots. Yet, in the end, none of that undid the vote. Joseph R. Biden won the 2020 presidential election.

A piece by the Brookings Institution, "How Black Americans Saved Biden and American Democracy," argues that black people did more than their share to elect the Democrat (Ray 2020). For instance, blacks* made up 12 percent of the population of Pennsylvania but 21 percent of Democratic voters. In Ohio, they made up 14 percent of the population but 21 percent of Democratic voters. But it is Georgia that took the cake, especially since it went from red to blue. Blacks made up 33 percent of the population of Georgia. They made up over 50 percent of Democratic voters in the state.

There is no doubt that the gallant efforts of former Georgia House Democratic leader Stacey Abrams and the organization she launched, Fair Fight (2020), as well as the activism of many other black women (Waxman 2021), put the Biden-Harris ticket over the edge. However, black religious leaders also played a critical role in the get-out-the-vote effort, as they have done for decades. They organized Souls to the Polls events and collaborated with political action committees and civic organizations across the country to mobilize the vote (Banks 2020).

What makes the involvement of black pastors so noteworthy, though this is often overlooked, is that they do this work on top of the myriad of responsibilities they already have as ministers. They are not only expected to be Bible scholars and teachers. When they speak, the audience is looking to hear words that motivate, heal, encourage, or inspire. Peo-

---

* Black and African American are used interchangeably throughout.

ple come to them for counsel on life's critical decisions and comfort during painful times. They are expected to officiate funerals, christenings, and weddings, among other important events, and for those who head churches, they need to be managers, strategists, and financial experts as well. This is true of all pastors. One white Catholic priest put it this way: "When we were in the seminary . . . we were taught theology, . . . you know, theology, scripture etc. We were never taught how to be a CEO or a CFO or an HR person . . . or a builder. You know . . . all of this, and then you just get thrust into it. . . . You have to be the fundraiser. . . . You have to manage the money. . . . You're in charge of everything; therefore, you're responsible for all the employees and everything."[1] Bottom line: ministers have a lot on their plates!

But for black ministers, these responsibilities take on a whole other meaning. Religion has been "the womb" of the black community in the United States, as Eric Lincoln and Lawrence Mamiya (1990) have noted. Expectations of black ministers in the United States, then, not only include having strong Bible knowledge, being good preachers, offering counseling services, performing important rituals, and in many cases running a 501(c)(3) but also often cultivating a sense of blackness, as a culture and identity, as well as carrying the mantel of leading black people through and out of racial oppression. They can approach this work, for example, through their sermon content, providing opportunities for economic development, socializing youth on how to navigate a racialized society, or facilitating spaces where black people can just, well . . . be black. Leading black people through and out of racial oppression can also be effected through mobilizing black people and others to challenge systems of white supremacy and black oppression. Indeed, many leaders for black freedom have been black ministers. Not all black ministers, perhaps not even most, have worked to help black people navigate a racially oppressive society. The black church and its ministers are not monolithic. But because of how religion is separated from the state in the US context as well as the historical centrality of black religious space for the black community more broadly, black ministers have had considerable agency to mobilize for social change, perhaps unlike any other institutionalized black leader in the United States.

Yet, as would be the case with any leader, black ministers who may want to be agents of social change must work within the constraints of broader macro-level contexts and with the tools available to them to do so. This book explores how black ministers negotiate this reality in the twenty-first century.

We want to first and foremost extend our sincere gratitude to the religious and civic leaders who graciously agreed to be interviewed for this book. They gave us their time and energy, resources in short supply considering all the demands placed on them. This study would not have been possible without their generosity. It is humbling when others place trust in you to tell a part of their story. We hope that this work honors the time and energy our respondents invested and the stories and perspectives they shared.

We have several others to acknowledge as well. We thank the Ruth Landes Memorial Research Fund, which provided financial resources that allowed us to conduct this research. This book has gone through many iterations and revisions. During that process, several of our colleagues provided helpful feedback and criticism, including J. Craig Jenkins and Andrew Martin. We are grateful for their careful review and comments. Also, we want to acknowledge the anonymous journal and book reviewers whose input helped us greatly as we refined our arguments and writing. We are grateful to the editor, Jennifer Hammer, for her insight and guidance in this process as well. Both authors also benefited from people in their personal lives who supported them throughout the years we were working on this book. Korie would like to thank her family for their patience, care, and support in the conducting and writing of this research, which took her away from family activities from time and time. Michelle would like to thank her family, including her husband Todd, stepson Riley, and parents Steve and Cindy Oyakawa, for their support while researching and writing this book.

Introduction

He was wearing a fitted, pewter-gray three-piece suit with a plaid black, white, and crimson dress shirt. The look was accented with a satiny crimson tie and matching pocket napkin. Behind him stood several other black men in similarly fine attire. This affable, smartly dressed pastor was being interviewed by a journalist with one of Ohio's local metro TV news programs about a protest he had organized. In response to the journalist's question about the protest, he replied,

> We want to do a demonstration of black excellence, and it is a prestigious protest against racism and injustice. We are having black men come out in their best attire. If you have a suit, we want you to come out suited and booted. If you don't have a suit, just put on your best. . . . We want to have a peaceful protest at City Hall . . . to express our frustration with the climate of America. (Sam 2020)

The purpose of the suits and ties, he explained, was "to debunk the disclaimer or the notion that we are some kind of threat to society." He continued: "The reality is we are productive citizens in all segments and sectors: doctors, lawyers, schoolteachers, news reporters. We are functioning in an excellent way on all levels of society, and we want to do a demonstration that speaks to that" (Sam 2020). The Demonstration of Black Excellence was a protest against police brutality and systemic racial injustice, and it aimed to prove to the world that black men are no threat to the United States. The subtext: black men, like all other men, are respectable and want nothing more than to contribute to the well-being of society. One could not help but connect their presentation to that of the iconic look of black pastors who led the civil rights movement of the 1950s and '60s. As the news reporter closed the segment, he noted, "They are taking it back in the day to the old days when they came out protesting with the suits and the ties on" (Sam 2020). This was June

2020. The Demonstration of Black Excellence was just one of several thousand Black Lives Matter (BLM) protests that organically erupted across not just the United States but the world. This Ohio city was not the only one where protests were organized for black men in suits and ties. They happened in cities in other parts of the United States as well (Rice 2020). Yet the Black Lives Matter movement was not birthed or sustained by black pastors in suits and ties, demonstrating black excellence. The credit for that goes to three black women, one of whom is queer (Black Lives Matter, n.d.), as well as many young people who took to the streets in anger, a good deal of them seemingly unaffiliated with any formal organization.

The BLM movement began in response to the murder of seventeen-year-old Trayvon Martin by George Zimmerman some eight years prior to the Demonstration of Black Excellence. Martin's murder stirred what was already an undercurrent of righteous indignation over the unjust murders of unarmed blacks. National media coverage has highlighted the deaths of Raymond Allen, Jordan Baker, Sean Bell, Sandra Bland, Duane Brown, Michael Brown, John Crawford III, Amadou Diallo, Ezell Ford, Eric Garner, Casey Goodson Jr., Oscar Grant, Freddie Gray, Akai Gurley, Eric Harris, Anthony Hill, Derrick Jones, Natasha McKenna, Tamir Rice, Tony Robinson, Walter Scott, and Philip White. Of course, there are countless others we do not know about. But it was not until the succession of the highly publicized murders of Ahmaud Arbery and then Breonna Taylor and then George Floyd that the Black Lives Matter movement was catapulted to new heights, becoming a multiracial, multiethnic, multigenerational global movement that spread from the United States to other countries including Australia, Sweden, Brazil, South Africa, Netherlands, France, Spain, Thailand, Japan, and South Korea, among many others (Liubchenkova 2020; DPA and Reuters 2020). The energy of the Black Lives Matter movement in the spring of 2020 was unlike any ever witnessed in recent history (Hart 2020). The black church, however, which was at the forefront of perhaps one of the most successful organic social movements in modern history, the civil rights movement, had been relatively inactive when it came to confronting the systemic killings of unarmed blacks, or any other systemic form of racial oppression of blacks for that matter, at least on a grand scale, since blacks began again to make inroads into politics in the 1980s.[1] This book provides clues as to why.

Drawing on the case of Ohio black religious leaders' voter-mobilization efforts leading up to the 2012 election, this book explores when, how, and why black religious leaders engage in broad-based mobilization in the twenty-first-century United States. While the political struggles that ensued during the 2012 presidential campaigns took place in battleground states all over the United States, there is one state that was of particular interest: Ohio. Ohio for decades was widely understood to be one of the more critical battleground states. No president since John F. Kennedy in 1960 had won the presidency without winning Ohio (D. Smith 2020). Reuters even proposed that the entire 2012 election might come down to a handful of counties in Ohio (Johnson 2012). The Barack Obama and Mitt Romney campaigns apparently believed Ohio was the critical path to the presidency as well. Ohio was the most visited state by both candidates. Both of their campaigns ran the most television ads there. And the Obama campaign located one in five of all of its campaign offices—nationwide—in Ohio. Ultimately, though, TV ads and campaign offices do not win states. Votes do.

President Barack Obama got the votes. He was reelected in 2012, securing a sizable majority (332) of the electoral votes. On the way, he won nine of the ten battleground states. And for the first time in US history, a greater proportion of the black electorate (66 percent) voted than the white electorate (64 percent) (Page and Overberg 2012). In hindsight, Obama's reelection may seem inevitable. Yet what might appear a foregone conclusion today was not so obvious prior to the 2012 election. Fueled by the Tea Party and what at best could be considered angst about the Affordable Care Act, a major disruption of the Democrats' political juggernaut occurred in the 2010 midterm elections. Republicans gained the power to influence if and when people could vote in states across the country and worked to institutionalize policies that threatened to constrain the suffrage of many groups (Balz 2010). Given voting patterns of previous elections, these changes were predicted to negatively and disproportionately affect the part of the electorate that tends to vote Democrat—especially African American churchgoers, who, where early voting days are instituted, traditionally vote after church on the Sunday before Election Day, a custom known as Souls to the Polls (T. Lee 2012). If there was one group that the Obama for America (OFA) campaign needed to come out big in 2012, it was African Americans. And there are no rival gatekeepers to this electorate than black religious leaders (see Harris 1999; Morris 1984; Pattillo-McCoy 1998).

For sure, religious leaders, regardless of their race, participate in various forms of political and civic engagement (Wuthnow 1999; Morris 1984; Wald 1989; Guth et al. 1997, 2003; Barnes 2004, 2005; Olson 2000; Crawford and Olson 2001; S. Lee 2003; McRoberts 2003; Pinn 2002; Shelton and Emerson 2012). But for black ministers in particular, civic and political engagement, in some form or another, is frequently seen as central to their role (Berenson, Elifson, and Tollerson 1976; Billingsley 1999; McDaniel 2003). Perhaps not surprisingly, religiously active African Americans, a large majority of whom attend churches headed by black ministers, are more likely to be civically and politically engaged than their less religious counterparts are (Fitzgerald and Spohn 2005; Reese, Brown, and Ivers 2007). And black congregations, particularly those affiliated with a black denomination, are more likely to be civically and politically engaged as well (Lincoln and Mamiya 1990; Barnes 2004, 2005). Barring a few notable exceptions (see McDaniel 2003; Barnes and Nwosu 2014), however, the analytic focus of most work exploring the relationship between religion and civic action among blacks is more on attendees or congregations, not the leaders of black religious organizations.

Contemporary social movement scholarship recognizes the importance of collaborative or complementary leadership strategies (Morris and Staggenborg 2007; Andrews et al. 2010; Lindsay 2008; Ganz 2009, 2010). This is really valuable work and has paid considerable dividends in outlining what a leader needs if they are to develop and guide a successful movement. In this book, however, we focus less on what it takes to be an effective leader of a social movement and the strategies one ought to employ to do so. Rather, this volume focuses on illuminating why and when black religious leaders become involved in social mobilization. In so doing, it helps inform why we see the mobilization that has occurred as well as why we have not seen more black religious leadership in the movements for black justice today, such as Black Lives Matter.

There has been some speculation about the capacity of contemporary black pastors to lead for social change.[2] Eddie Glaude Jr. pointedly questions the prophetic relevancy of the black church in his opinion piece "The Black Church Is Dead" (2012). But is the black church dead? Can black religious leaders today do what so many of their counterparts collectively achieved in generations past? They can. They can indeed mobilize, and they can do so effectively and efficiently for a sustained amount of time (at least a year) over a large geographic area, in the case of this book, a state. Black religious leaders across Ohio mobilized the black vote in 2012 (Page and Overberg 2013).

This begs the question, if black religious leaders could collectively mobilize on a broad scale for the black vote, why have they not done so for black lives? One might argue that they are opposed to some of the values of the Black Lives Matter organization. The gender and sexuality ideology of some black religious leaders might hinder their willingness to be linked with BLM, which affirms fluid understandings of gender and sexuality. But in that instance, black religious leaders could still mobilize for black lives and against police brutality separate from the official BLM organization. It is common for movements to have multiple organizations working toward the same general aims (Fernandez and McAdam 1988). Strikingly, the black religious leaders in this study were not collectively mobilizing for black lives in any capacity.

This book argues that there are several factors that together help to explain why. One is the enduring legacy of the civil rights movement. The black religious leaders in our study maintain a nostalgic reverence for the civil rights movement era. There is a high value placed on civil rights movement actions and achievements and its pastor leaders. This legacy continues to powerfully shape the identity of today's black religious leaders and their culture. It is perhaps the most central organizing feature of the black religious leader community. To be a black religious leader is to reflect the iconic civil rights movement pastor. This clear sense of what it means to be a black religious leader reinforces a deeper sense of mutuality and interdependence among black religious leaders. Yet, ironically, a key challenge is that the cultural tools passed on through the civil rights movement legacy may constrain black religious leaders' capacity to address black oppression today.

Additionally, a number of black religious leaders adhere to what we call the *black Protestant ethic*. This moral framework is partially rooted in a white Western Protestantism that emphasizes black responsibility and individual accountability and places the onus of addressing existing disadvantages on blacks. This ethic hinders an investment in broad mobilization efforts that resist structural racism.

The civil rights movement legacy and black Protestant ethic are internal to the black religious leader community. There are two additional factors external to black religious leaders that impact when, how, and why they mobilize on a broader scale as well. One has to do with their relationship with black-centered civic organizations (e.g., the National Association for the Advancement of Colored People [NAACP], the Southern Christian Leadership Conference [SCLC]) and faith-based community organizations (FBCOs). Over the past four decades, the role of the SCLC and NAACP has seemed to decline, while FBCOs have consumed increasingly more space in the social movement field (Wood, Fulton, and Partridge 2012). The PICO network (now called Faith in Action), for instance, which originated in 1972, has a presence in at least 150 cities nationwide and has engaged over one thousand congregations in local and national mobilization activities (Pico Network, n.d.). The growing presence of these kinds of organizations has changed how social mobilization is done (Wood, Fulton, and Partridge 2012). This transformation has had at least two implications for the efforts of contemporary black religious leaders.

The expansion of FBCOs since the 1970s means that black religious leaders have other options for mobilizing. The FBCO is an ecumenical, racially diverse organizing model that takes on social justice issues. This is appealing to many black religious leaders. However, the FBCO model differs in important ways from that of the civil rights movement model. The civil rights movement model is religiously ecumenical (at least within Christianity), but it is led by African Americans and focuses on issues particularly germane to the lives of African Americans. FBCOs, on the other hand, are often led by white people and rely on white institutions for their funding. They may still pursue goals relating to racial justice, but many of their campaigns do not center on the black community. When black religious leaders devote their resources to these kinds of organizations, it undercuts their ability to mobilize on behalf of specifically African American causes. In a very real sense, FBCOs compete for the resources that black religious leaders control. This includes their personal resources, such as their time, energy, and ideas. It also includes the resources connected to their churches, such as people who would be volunteer activists, as well building space, administrative and technological resources, and funds. Opportunities to engage in an

FBCO means these resources can be divided and diffused and thereby be less available for endeavors organized by the black religious leader community. Still, FBCOs may be the best game in town for black ministers to collectively mobilize for social change if this is something they want to pursue.

The second external factor is how post-civil-rights-era racism contributes to the likelihood and form of black religious leader collective action. It is important to account for race in our understanding of black religious leaders' mobilization for at least two reasons. Successful social movements have to develop frames that are both consistent with and disruptive of the dominant ideology (Benford and Snow 2000; Rochefort and Cobb 1993). This is no easy task. But black religious leaders, really up through the civil rights movement, were able to do this by relying on narratives that were explicitly racial, in large part, because the structures being confronted were very much racially framed. Post-civil-rights-era racial ideology, however, while remaining effective at sustaining the racial hierarchy, largely depends on implicit racism and indirect racial discrimination. In recent years, we have seen an increase in explicit, bold racist rhetoric. As the BLM movement gained momentum, the rhetoric increased all the more. This, in combination with the systemic racism laid bare by COVID-19 and the successive murders of Arbery, Taylor, and Floyd at a moment when people across the world had little to divert their attention from these atrocities, is perhaps why the BLM movement took off in 2020. Americans could no longer easily turn a blind eye to racism. Yet the reality remains that the racism of today is largely implicit, baked into how the United States does life. The civil rights movement legacy that informs the identity and culture of black religious leaders and their community is one that challenged Jim Crow, an explicitly racist discriminatory system. The challenge for contemporary movement leaders, regardless of race or religious affiliation, is developing effective mobilization frames that undermine and expose covert white supremacy.

Together, these four factors have important implications for what, how, and why black religious leaders mobilize, impacting the capacity and form of their mobilization efforts in the twenty-first-century United States and shedding light on the challenges they may face in mobilizing on behalf of the black community.

Black Church, Leadership, and Civic and Political Engagement

There is little doubt that there is a link between religion and civic and political engagement (Verba, Lehman, and Brady 1995; Beyerlein and Chaves 2003).[3] Indeed, religion is part and parcel to the civic and political activism of African Americans (Cook and Wilcox 1990; Baer and Singer 1992; Harris 1999; Lincoln and Mamiya 1990; Brown and Brown 2003; Brown 2006; Cavendish 2002; Chaves and Higgins 1992), at least among those who are in Generation X or older. Compared to other congregations, African American congregations affiliated with black denominations, like the African Methodist Episcopal or National Baptist Convention, are particularly likely to engage in this sort of activism (Brown 2006; Cavendish 2002; Chaves and Higgins 1992; Beyerlein and Chaves 2003). In many ways, this is because black church culture serves as a primary source for organizing and developing frames for African Americans' civic and political engagement (McAdam 1982; Morris 1984; Pattillo-McCoy 1998). Attendees of black congregations, particularly those affiliated with black denominations, are exposed to an "oppositional civic culture" that offers alternative views and norms that challenge the hegemonic structure (Harris 1999). Still, this is not always the case. Omar McRoberts (2003), in his study of black congregations in a predominantly black and poor Boston neighborhood, finds that their community activism is personalized, largely constructed by congregants and clergy as meeting individuals' material and spiritual needs and less about challenging systemic racism.

Additionally, we know that head clergy, across lines of race and religious tradition, engage in political activities, advocating for political candidates and using their pulpits to affect members' views about social and political issues (Djupe and Gilbert 2002; Guth et al. 1997; Smidt 2003; G. Smith 2005; Crawford and Olson 2001). Black religious leaders have often played a critical role in cultivating and nurturing activism within the black community. Indeed, some of the most iconic leaders of civic and political activism in the black community have been religious leaders. Richard Allen, Nat Turner, C. H. Mason, Dr. Martin Luther King Jr., and Malcolm X are just a few examples. Black women activists, like Ida B. Wells and Fannie Lou Hamer, while not officially religious leaders, drew heavily on their Christian faith in their resistance to white supremacy. Yet their efforts cannot be understood separate from their contexts. Eric McDaniel, in *Politics in the Pews: The Political Mobilization of Black Churches* (2008), argues that the political participation of black religious organizations is primarily dependent on two factors: the mutual interests of head clergy and their attendees, and the politicization of the social context.

Black religious leaders as well as their churches continue to be actively engaged in social, civic, and political activism. There is variation across black churches and clergy, of course. Furthermore, just because a church is made up of mostly black people and has a minister who is black does not mean it will be "down for the cause." Even still, black clergy and their churches, by and large, maintain a voice of resistance even today (Barnes and Nwosu 2014). Relative to white religious leaders, they are more structural in their social orientations (Shelton and Emerson 2012), and they are inclined toward progressive politics and activism (Baumann 2016).

Leadership and Mobilization

For nearly four decades, resource mobilization (Jenkins 1983; Cress and Snow 1996; Ganz 2000; A. Martin 2008) and political process perspectives (McAdam 1982; Tarrow 1994; Tilly 1978) have dominated social movement scholarship. The resource mobilization perspective (McCarthy and Zald 1977) argues that the capacity of a social movement organization (SMO) to gather and mobilize resources is essential to achieving its aims. The political process perspective places a good deal of emphasis on acting when the right political opportunity emerges (McAdam 1982; Tarrow 1994; Tilly 1978). A central thesis of this work is that factors external to social movements play an important role in movement success (Kitschelt 1986; Meyer and Minkoff 2004).

There are more recent studies that call into question the importance of political processes, finding the impact of political opportunity to be limited (Banaszak 1996; McCammon 2001; Ganz 2009). These other lines of research refocus attention on processes internal to social movements, like cultural framing (Benford and Snow 2000; Snow et al. 1986) and collective identity formation (Polletta and Jasper 2001; Bernstein 2005). Framing and collective identity are critical for social mobilization because they motivate participation and promote cohesion among movement participants (Friedman and McAdam 1992; Polletta and Jasper 2001; Hunt and Benford 2004). In the civil rights movement, for instance, black religious leaders provided culturally resonant frames that mobilized the black community and appealed to sympathetic publics (Morris 1984). Other factors to consider have to do with how people feel about an issue and their level of motivation to get involved (Klandermans and Oegema 1987).

Scholarship on social mobilization and leadership is relatively limited as compared to these other streams of research. Still, there is a growing interest in leadership of social mobilization (Morris 2000; Barker, Johnson, and Lavalette 2001). Existing work in this area tends to emphasize collective leadership or teams of leaders and how they construct strategy. Strategy and direction emerge out of a dialogical process among a group of people (Andrews et al. 2010; Lindsay 2008; Ganz 2009, 2010). Barbara Ryan (2001) notes this dynamic in the suffragist movement in Ireland, for example, which was composed of many leaders of several small networks of women who represented multiple constituencies with quite divergent interests. Marshall Ganz (2010), in his work on the farm workers' movement in California, similarly highlights the importance of teams of leaders. He argues that social movements need to have leaders with diverse but culturally relevant backgrounds to build what he calls "strategic capacity," which is a group's ability to be creative and innovate against more powerful opponents. Aldon Morris and Suzanne Staggenborg (2007) outline separate tiers of leadership in mobilization. They argue that these tiers represent varying leadership types, all of which are necessary for the execution of social movements.

Not only does research emphasize the importance of collective leadership, but it also notes the importance of having the right people on leadership teams to craft strategies that are innovative and relevant to the mobilization context. Implicit in this is that someone needs to get the right people into the room. Michael Lindsay (2008), based on his study of elite evangelicals, calls this "convening power," the ability to bring influential leaders of disparate groups together. This power matters, because it is not until leaders are convened that they can collectively produce narratives, strategies, and plans for future collaboration.

Social mobilization scholars know that leaders are important. They emphasize what leaders do to gather resources and build movements (McCarthy and Wolfson 1996); how leaders work together (Ganz 2009; Andrews et al. 2010; Baggetta, Han, and Andrews 2013); how leaders make choices about mobilization strategies (A. Martin 2007; Han 2014); and the varying types of leaders that emerge in movements (Morris and Staggenborg 2007). The aim of existing work, though, is to understand what factors affect social movements. Leadership is presented as just one of many factors contributing to the effectiveness of social movements. We propose that leadership demands particular attention as a social phenomenon that is beyond factors that produce effective social movements. It is leaders who decide what issues to pursue and how to pursue them. They also are the ones who can garner sufficient resources to do the work. Looking at who the leaders actually are can provide insights into what they will do and, just as important, why they will do it.

The Racial Environment

It is tempting to see today's racial environment as being fundamentally different than it was in 2012. The rhetoric of Donald Trump and other political figures makes it seem as though racism has once again become normalized in public discourse. But, in reality, the white-supremacist rhetoric that the public has been subjected to over recent years is, as Lawrence Bobo suggests, simply a different manifestation of "the continuing and durable power of race and racial prejudice in our national politics and political discourse" (2017, S86). It is not a diversion from a path toward postracialism because the United States was never, in fact, on a postracism path. The racist rhetoric of Trump and his allies is in its intent and outcome consistent with the racism (albeit more covert) that undergirded the US racial landscape during President Obama's era. But Americans are not particularly comfortable with such openly racist attitudes and actions. Between 2011 and 2017, for instance, the Pew Research Center reports that the percentage of people who said that racism is a "big problem" increased from 28 percent to 58 percent (Neal 2017). The preferred approach is one that eschews explicit racism and racist rhetoric while overlooking persistent racial inequality and institutionalized racism.

There are various conceptualizations that have been put forth to explain post-civil-rights-era racism. Each grapples with how to understand the decline in overt racism and the simultaneous persistence of attitudes, behaviors, and systems that reaffirm the racial hierarchy. Donald Kinder and David Sears, for instance, propose "symbolic racism," which they say is a "blend of anti-black affect and the kind of traditional American moral values embodied in the Protestant Ethic" (1981, 416). They suggest that contemporary racism is less about racial threat and more about childhood socialization. John Dovidio and Samuel Gaertner's "aversive racism" is "the conflict between whites' personal prejudice and underlying unconscious negative feelings toward and beliefs about blacks" (2004, 4). Aversive racists may even be egalitarian in their worldview. They envelop their racism in a more prowhite orientation than an antiblack one to avoid any stigma associated with being seen as racially prejudiced.

Whereas symbolic racism and aversive racism are social psychological explanations for post-civil-rights-era racism, laissez-faire racism and colorblind racism are sociological. Laissez-faire racism is a form of institutional racism in which "longstanding values of meritocracy, individualism, majority rule and competition in a free marketplace . . . weave together as rationalization for persistent racial inequality in a putatively anti-discrimination, race-neutral democratic state" (Bobo 2017, S91). It is informed by Herbert Blumer's theory of race prejudice as a sense of group position, which says that racial prejudice is about the dominant racial group developing a racial frame that will reinforce its superior status. For Lawrence Bobo, James Kluegel, and Ryan Smith (1996), laissez-faire racism is a way of maintaining dominance in an era when overt racism is no longer necessary or preferable to the covert form. And then, Eduardo Bonilla-Silva (2003) proposes "colorblind racism," which focuses on stories that most whites tell themselves and others to justify the existing racial hierarchy that privileges whites. Colorblind racism is mainly distinguishable from laissez-faire racism in its emphasis on "whites' racial discourse as the racial ideology of the dominant race rather than as 'prejudice' (individuals' affective dispositions)" (Bonilla-Silva, Lewis, and Embrick 2004, 561). Bonilla-Silva and his colleagues see survey data as being limited as a method for understanding racism because "the issue is not to identify the proportion of 'racist' individuals in the population who subscribe to prejudiced views" (Bonilla-Silva, Lewis, and Embrick 2004, 561). Qualitative data, interviews in particular, are better suited to reveal the subtle yet powerful ways that whites make sense of a racial hierarchy that persistently privileges them.

These conceptualizations use different theoretical frames and competing claims about how to best measure racism in today's United States. Suffice it to say, the racism of the post-civil-rights United States is difficult to capture, largely because it has the uncanny ability to be effective while still indirect and implicit. If race scholars continue to grapple with the racism of today, it should be expected that black religious leaders would as well. They are often expected to deconstruct modern-day racism. This is on top of the expectation that they figure out what that means for them as religious leaders of people who remain, in many ways, at the bottom of the racial hierarchy and experience the effects of a racist social structure on a daily basis. If black religious leaders want to mobilize against racist structures, this can present a real challenge.

The Case

This book focuses on a multimethod qualitative case study of black religious leaders in Ohio. It relies on selecting a theoretically informed case. It draws on fifty-four in-depth interviews with black religious leaders and civic organization leaders in Ohio. It also incorporates observations of civic activities in which black religious leaders were key participants as well as content analysis of public documents. The study was conducted in a historically important moment. The first and only black president was up for reelection. Additionally, state governments across the country were changing or aiming to change voting opportunities in ways that would negatively and disproportionately affect African Americans. Ohio was no exception (Gomez 2019). Access to the vote really mattered in Ohio, one of several battleground states at the time (J. Martin 2012). And on top of this, the Black Lives Matter movement was just gaining steam. The timing of the study captured a moment when black religious leaders were presented with unique issues to mobilize for, ones that would matter a lot for the lives of many blacks in the United States. It also was a moment when broad, collective social action by black religious leaders in the state was evident. We took advantage of that moment. (See the appendix for more on methodology.)

Looking Ahead

This book describes a case in which contemporary black religious leaders' collective participation in civic and political action had implications beyond the local level, and it theorizes about the social processes that impact when, how, and why they participate in these activities in a society where, by and large, racism and its effects are covert and implicit. We aim to extend knowledge of (1) leadership of social movements, (2) the black church and broad-based social mobilization in the post-civil-rights era, and (3) the influence of dominant racial ideology on contemporary mobilization efforts of black religious leaders. In the following chapters, we address our central research aims from various angles. All names for people are pseudonyms. In most cases, names for organizations are pseudonyms as well. There is one exception. In chapter 5, which looks at black pastors' involvement in civic and community organizations, the actual names of organizations are almost always used.

1

On the Front Lines

It was a cold, dreary November day. But you would not know it from the energy amid one of Ohio's county board of elections polling sites, this one a former stand-alone department store turned into an election site. It was Souls to the Polls Sunday, and the parking lot was filled to capacity. Drivers drove up and down the lanes of the parking lot searching for newly opened spots. And while the election site may have been officially bipartisan, anyone present that day knew this was Obamaland.

Obama for America (OFA) had set up a booth at the back of the parking lot. Party music, mixed by a twenty-something, hip-looking black DJ, blared from the large speakers flanking the OFA table. Throughout the parking lot, there was a diverse bunch of no less than fifteen volunteers—white, black, young, middle-aged, women, men. But most were white middle-aged women and young adults in their early twenties or younger. Some of the volunteers worked at the OFA table passing out campaign materials and answering questions. Others walked around passing out fliers to people in line. And others directed people to the end of the voter line. This job was needed. The line was equivalent to about four blocks long. With no more room along the front and side of the building, voters had turned the line in on itself and began to extend the line into the parking lot, where it formed into a spiral. Then there were the women dressed from head to toe in rented Sesame Street–character costumes. They hung out on the sidewalk adjacent to the parking lot, shouting and jumping around while holding pro-Democrat signs in a seeming attempt to draw attention to the location of the election site and make a last-ditch pitch to voters to vote Democrat. The one Romney campaigner, a middle-aged white man roaming the parking lot handing out fliers, was indeed in enemy territory.[1]

Souls to the Polls Sunday was not the main strategy that black religious leaders in Ohio engaged in to mobilize voters in 2012. They employed a host of activities. If the data from this study are any indication, nearly all of them urged their congregants, beginning several months prior to Election Day, to register to vote and to vote early. A majority facilitated voter registration, arranging time and space for people to register at their churches. A sizable minority ensured that their churches provided daily transportation to county boards of elections for people to register to vote. Some set up voter-registration verification clinics at their churches, where people could check whether they were registered to vote and then register right there if they were not. Others held education forums, which taught people how to fill out and submit provisional and absentee ballots. Several black religious leaders hosted OFA campaign surrogates, including the singer John Legend and the actor Lawrence Fishburne, permitting them to speak during worship services. And some allowed their churches to be used as polling places. The energy, passion, and engagement of Ohio black religious leaders during the 2012 election cycle was palpable and abrogated any questions we had entertained until then about the capacity of black leaders and their churches to mobilize and effect change. The black church, at least in Ohio, was by no means dead (see Glaude 2012).

In this chapter, we tell the story of how Ohio black religious leaders made sense of why it was important to mobilize the vote in 2012. Any time a leader wants to get others to follow them, they have to provide a compelling reason to those whom they want to mobilize why they ought to act. This is called *framing*. Frames are critical to any social mobilization effort (Benford and Snow 2000; Snow et al. 1986). They communicate to potential followers that what is going on matters, that the events people are witnessing or experiencing are meaningful (Benford and Snow 2000, 614), that they are not ordinary, that they are not acceptable.

Not all frames are effective. Effective frames resonate with people (Snow and Benford 1988) and motivate them to want to act. They have to tap into who people are or how they see themselves or who they want to be. Then, they have to continually be kept at the forefront of the minds of people who are active in movements to maintain momentum (Benford and Snow 2000, 613). People who lead mobilization efforts play a critical role here. If they cannot make sense of events in a way that resonates with people and motivates them to follow them, if they cannot keep that message in front of the people they hope to mobilize, then they will not be able to get the movement off the ground and sustained.

Not surprisingly, black religious leaders in our study were motivated to reelect President Barack Obama. He was the first US president who identified as black. He is married to a black woman. His pastor for twenty years, Rev. Jeremiah Wright, was a leading social-justice-oriented black pastor in Chicago. On the surface, any one of these reasons seems sufficient to motivate blacks in the pews to get out the black vote in 2012. But none of them was the reason black religious leaders in our study gave for why it was important to vote or mobilize the vote.

There is perhaps good reason for this. The luster of having a black president began to wane some by 2012. President Obama's approval rating had slipped by eight percentage points among blacks between 2009 and 2011, from 93 percent to 85 percent (Jones 2011). This is still a very high approval rating. But such slippage forecasted that blacks would not be as motivated to vote as they were during President Obama's first presidential campaign. The decline in support signaled trouble for people invested in reelecting President Obama.

Meanwhile, there had been a major disruption of the Democrats' political juggernaut during the 2010 midterm elections. Democrats controlled twenty-seven state governments prior to the midterms. After the elections, they only controlled seventeen, and the Republicans had taken over twenty-six, including Ohio (Balz 2010). The Republicans gained the power to influence if and when people could vote in states across the country. They took advantage of their good fortunes in the midterm elections and attempted to implement laws in battleground states across the country that would primarily restrict the voting opportunities of Democratic voters. In Ohio, for instance, one of the main strategies of the Republican Party, led by its Republican secretary of state, Jon Husted, was to severely restrict early voting. The plan aimed to eliminate Souls to the Polls Sunday. If put into effect, it would have disproportionately disenfranchised African Americans and furthered Republicans' chances to take the White House in 2012. Yet, by doing this, Republicans (unbeknownst to them) offered black religious leaders the perfect gift in all their zeal to change voting access: a mobilization frame. The move to try to disenfranchise blacks at that moment in history proved to be a major political misstep.

The Ohio black religious leaders who were at the forefront of the get-out-the-vote effort understood their role, and they seized on this misstep, constructing what proved to be an effective frame to mobilize their followers. They told followers that the attempted changes to voting laws were akin to Jim Crow–era tactics of black oppression, manifestations of modern-day racism. This frame worked to motivate not only churchgoers but also other black religious leaders across denominational affiliations who had not yet committed to action.

It Is Time to Act

The summer before the election, the presiding bishop of the Church of God in Christ (COGIC) wrote a letter imploring bishops, directors, and pastors in the denomination to get engaged in local voter-mobilization efforts. In this online letter, he asked people to participate in two national events organized by the denomination: National Voter Registration Weekend and National Absentee Ballot Weekend. Here is an excerpt from the letter:

> August 24–26: National Voter Registration Weekend
> All COGIC congregations are asked to identify unregistered voters within their congregations, provide support in registering eligible voters and submitting voter registration forms to the proper authorities after the weekend.
>
> October 26–28: National Absentee Ballot Weekend
> All COGIC congregations are asked to identify persons that will not be available to vote on Election Day and ensure that absentee ballots are properly completed and turned in to the proper authorities after the weekend. Please place a high priority on this initiative to maximize its effectiveness. For additional information and resources on the electoral process and the initiative, please visit www.cogic.org.
> Developing consciences for the absentee ballot initiative is urgent. Please share this letter with pastors/churches in your area. [Our denomination] cannot relinquish its socio-political responsibility for the common good and we must continue our goal of nurturing enthusiasm for the electoral process and to reach out to all eligible voters among our constituents. (Blake 2012)

The COGIC presiding bishop did not equivocate about the importance of bishops' and pastors' engagement in voter mobilization. He urged all leaders in the denomination to participate in several mobilization strategies aimed at getting people registered to vote and, once registered, getting them to vote early. This was an "urgent" matter. Battles over access to the vote were being waged in many key political states across the country. The presiding bishop and the national COGIC board were surely aware of this and the potential impact of any changes on black voters. The reason given for such urgency was quite vague and perhaps intentionally so. The claim was that the denomination had a responsibility to make sure that it supported efforts that helped the common good, and that included making sure people participated in the electoral process. The presiding bishop's call for participation avoided any hint of racism and politics. We surmise that as the top leader of a national organization, he chose careful wording to avoid any potential legal ramifications associated with violating the separation of church and state while also signaling concerns about voter-suppression tactics.

Within three months after this letter was posted, the COGIC bishops of Ohio, however, made it abundantly clear that pastors under their jurisdiction were expected to engage in get-out-the-vote efforts. It was September. By this time, the struggle to prevent the secretary of state, John Husted, from eliminating Souls to the Polls Sunday was under way. Unlike national leadership, the pastors were very clear about their concerns. In some respects, they needed to be. Ohio was on the front lines of the battle. The challenges to the black vote, if put into effect, would directly impact people in their pews and in the wider community.

Fourteen Ohio COGIC bishops appeared in a press conference to announce whose side of the battle they were on and how they would combat the threats to voting access in the state. It was clearly choreographed in advance, from what to wear to how and where they would sit or stand. The bishops, all men at least middle-aged (several appeared much older), were uniformly dressed. Eleven wore clerical garb, black overcoats with purple or black clergy shirts. The other three wore black suits with white shirts and neutral-colored ties. Their clothing communicated their status as clergy, that they were men to be respected, and the color coordination told the viewer they were a unified front in this endeavor.

The bishops were arranged in two rows, five seated at a table and the others standing behind them. The bishop who sat in the center of the five at the table made the announcement. He said,

> The Ohio Churches of God in Christ is here to announce a statewide initiative to register, educate and turn out voters for the upcoming 2012 election. Now this initiative, getting souls to the polls, is designed to answer unprecedented restrictions on ballot access and increase civic participation among the Churches of God in Christ members. Churches of God in Christ was founded in 1907 and is the nation's largest Pentecostal denomination. . . . Bishop Floyd Perry quoted in [the] past Dr. Martin Luther King Jr. [who] called voting the foundation stone for political action. Sadly . . . we have seen that foundation weaken in recent years due to voter suppression and other intimidation tactics. The Ohio Churches of God in Christ coalition of bishops is committed to ensuring that everyone with the right to vote in Ohio has the ability to exercise that right.

Compared to the national COGIC statement, the Ohio COGIC bishops' call to mobilize the vote left no doubt in the minds of their audience why they were engaged. For them, voter mobilization was not about the common good, as the national presiding bishop said in his letter, but about exposing attempts by the state to suppress the vote and intimidate eligible voters. The Ohio government stood accused of trying to revert to Jim Crow–era strategies of oppression. Ohioans' access to the vote, especially that of blacks in the state, was at stake. This was a very real and tangible threat. Evoking Dr. Martin Luther King Jr., the bishops aligned their cause with the legacy of the civil rights movement. They linked their urgent call to the freedom struggle of blacks. Voter mobilization was about protecting black people's rights.

COGIC was not the only black denomination that used its institutional structure to mobilize the vote across the state. Another black denomination[2] took advantage of its annual regional meetings of pastors and lay leaders to do so. Less than two weeks before Election Day, I (the lead author) attended one of these meetings, which was held at the church of one of the denomination's pastors. The meeting lasted all day and took place in the sanctuary, which I estimated to be able to seat at least three hundred people. I arrived at 7:45 a.m. And when I left at 8:30 p.m., the program had still not ended.

It was a miserable, rainy, cold day. When the meeting started, a quarter past 8:00 a.m., there were only about twenty-five people present, which may have been because of the bad weather or the hot breakfast still being served in the church basement. The first item on the agenda was singing and worship. The song leaders repeatedly attempted to lead the people in the pews in several gospel hymns, but to no avail. Just a few people sang and clapped along with them. It was quite an uncomfortable scene, as the song leaders were working very hard to get people to "praise the Lord" in song with very few people obliging their pleas.

By the time the get-out-the-vote session got under way, which was next on the agenda, there were about a hundred people in the sanctuary. Although all were black, it was a somewhat diverse group of people present. About two-thirds of the people were women, and those present were disproportionately older. The average age I guessed to be about late fifties, and a number of people looked to be in their seventies or eighties. Everyone was dressed up: suits, shirts and ties, dresses, two-piece suits with skirts, heels, hats. I was grateful that I went with my three-piece gray pant suit and heels that day. Even then, I felt a tad underdressed and perhaps a little plain.

The lackluster participation of people in worship stood in direct contrast to their engagement in the get-out-the-vote session. It was like the get-out-the-vote session was the main event of a concert, and the worship was just the opening act. Whereas the song leaders could barely get people to open their mouths, the speakers at the get-out-the-vote session enjoyed considerable response, with "Amens" being said throughout the session. Person after person would get up to ask speakers questions or offer their own insight about what was going on with voting in the state. And when there were times of near silence, it was only because of the rapt attention audience members were paying to speakers.

The main focus of the session was a panel that addressed get-out-the-vote efforts in the state. There were five people on the panel, four men and one woman, all black. Mark Thompson, a seasoned activist, pastor, and leader in a national civic organization, was on the panel. There was also a state congressman. One of the men was with Voters First, a group that aimed to change the way electoral districts were determined in

Ohio. The woman was formerly active in the labor union and was now a dedicated volunteer with OFA. The final panelist was a pastor with the denomination who was also a leader in a local faith-based community organization. Mark Thompson, though, was the star that day. He provided the narrative for voting early, linking it to the historical struggle of blacks' right to vote in the United States.

Thompson, dressed in a two-piece suit with shirt and tie, stood up from his seat and walked toward the congregation, taking a few steps up the center aisle of the sanctuary for effect. And it worked. It grabbed my attention and, I suspect, others' too. It was also helpful that Thompson was a big man, at least six feet tall and with some girth around his middle section.

He got to the point. People needed to vote and vote early! Like the Ohio COGIC bishops, he tied his pleas to the legacy of the civil rights movement and the fight against voter suppression during that era. He then pulled on the heartstrings with a story laced with nostalgia. Thompson reminded us that his "granddaddy" and others in that generation treated Election Day like a holiday. It was even referred to as "Sacred Tuesday," he explained. People would put on their best clothes to go down to the polls to vote, he told the audience. And then, he said, there was Super Sunday, the Sunday before Election Day. On that day, people would get in their cars right after church and drive straight to the polls to vote early. But what Thompson really wanted the audience to take away from his story was that this approach was no longer going to work. Early voting could no longer be put off to Super Sunday like it was during his granddaddy's generation. That would not work if they were going to make a difference in this current environment of voter suppression. "No more!" he shouted. "No more of that. We need to vote early. We need to vote now! We need to vote every day of the week!" By this time, he had taken more purposeful steps up the center aisle. His voice had raised, and he was leaning forward, his fist lifted in the air to emphasize his points. He brought to the audience's attention the urgency of the moment, that these challenges to voting opportunities in the state were simply another strategy to suppress the black vote, a right for which those who came before fought so hard. He shouted, "They have awakened a sleeping lion!" His message: they will pay, if we vote early—now!

The denomination's regional director, Pastor Leonard Winston, had been seated in a high-back wooden chair on the stage at the front of the sanctuary during the entire session, with his wife seated next to him. Winston was dressed in a well-fitted, three-piece, dark pinstriped suit, shirt, and tie. He had a personable, outgoing way about him. After the panel was finished, he got up from his seat and declared, "This is a wonderful panel. Wonderful panel. It was great, and I appreciate them coming out!" Winston looked to be well into his sixties. While Pastor Winston was applauding the panel, Mrs. Winston stood up next to her husband and reminded him to announce that there will be a region-wide time of prayer and fasting right before the election. She was dressed in a two-piece white suit with a skirt. Pastor Winston did as she asked, giving the dates of the prayer and fasting. But, right after announcing the fast, he stressed in a louder tone, "And vote! Pray, fast, and vote!" I suppose, for Pastor Winston, fasting and praying were good, but voting was even better. Faith without works is dead.

Mrs. Winston then took the microphone after her husband was done and invited a twenty-something-looking woman to come up to the front. She was seated in the back of the sanctuary, so it took some time for her to get to the front of the church, which produced a level of antici-pation. What was she going to do? Impressively, the young woman had memorized and recited the entirety of a speech by Rev. Dr. William Bar-ber II, delivered at the 2012 NAACP national convention (DLVideos100 2012). In keeping with the theme of the session, the speech stressed the urgency of voting now, an act that has historical implications. It linked the current threats to voting opportunities across the country not only to the legacy of the civil rights movement but also to blacks' journey toward freedom from slavery to the election of Obama. It reminded the listener of the heroes and martyrs of freedom movements gone by. Bib-lical people such as Esther, Moses, Daniel, and David were mentioned, as well as African Americans like Frederick Douglass, Harriet Tubman, Medgar Evers, and Trayvon Martin. Challenges to freedom and the final victories achieved were repeatedly highlighted. These included the Civil War and the Emancipation Proclamation, the murder of Emmett Till, Bloody Sunday, the passage of the Voting Rights Act, and the election of Barack Obama to the US presidency. It was imperative that the legacy of freedom not be undone. And voting was how people could stand against modern threats to suffrage today. The speech and the woman's delivery of it were deeply moving and inspiring.

After this, the get-out-the-vote session ended. But lest someone in the audience still did not get the message, there was yet one more reminder of the urgency of getting out the vote early now. During the break between sessions, Pastor Winston asked a woman to sing a song called "Let My People Vote." It was sung to the tune of the black spiritual "Go Down Moses" (better known as "Let My People Go"). She stood in front of the church and sang, with conviction. As she progressed through the song, you could hear the people in the pews begin to join her in the chorus. The lyrics of the song are,

VERSE 1
When Satan tried to block our way
Let my people vote.
Our voice he tried to take away
Let my people vote.

CHORUS
Go down, to the polls, in Ohio
Tell those pharaohs to let my people vote.

VERSE 2
They thought that we would stay away
Let my people vote
We'll let them know we're here to stay
Let my people vote
We'll let them know we're here to stay
Let my people vote[3]

The get-out-the-vote session had one aim—get people to vote early and get them to mobilize other people to vote early. Considerable time was set aside educating people about the logistics of making sure people's votes counted. But what was critically important, and those who organized this event clearly knew this, was the reason why people needed to mobilize. Simply telling people to vote early was not going to work. There needed to be a why behind the plea. Thompson telling people about his granddaddy's generation and Super Sunday and the young woman reciting Rev. Barber's NAACP speech gave those who were present the social, spiritual, and cultural reasons to get engaged. They invigorated the crowd. But "Let My People Vote" brought the message home to Ohio. This was not a distant, universal, vague call to action. The fight for freedom was not far off somewhere else. It was right there. Ohio was on the front lines of a battle being waged against hard-won freedoms for which ancestors had labored, even died, for over a span of hundreds of years. People were being enlisted in this battle. Voting was not only a spiritual weapon to be deployed against the forces of evil but a civic weapon to be deployed against political forces. People must follow Moses's example and stand up to agents of power that would prevent them from doing God's will. They must follow the example of black Americans before and hold claim to the American birthright for which they fought and sometimes died. It was in their hands to protect the legacy. Mobilizing the vote was how this army could do it.

Mobilization Theater

Souls to the Polls, or Super Sunday, as Thompson's grandparents referred to it, is the Sunday before Election Day. Despite Thompson's plea, however, it did still matter. Considerable energy was put into getting people to vote on Souls to the Polls Sunday. Black religious leaders left no stone unturned to make sure their efforts paid off. This was evident at the Souls to the Polls activities at the department store that had been turned into the county board of elections. The presence of black religious leaders and church members there was not just about getting out the vote. Their presence also held symbolic significance. That day was when their efforts and those of their congregations could be seen, not just by them but by the world.

Before heading to the county board of elections, I (the lead author) attended a Souls to the Polls event of a small, largely upper-middle-class, African American church affiliated with a mainline Protestant denomination. When I arrived, worship service had ended, and a catered lunch was under way. My sponsor at the event, who attended the church and was actively engaged in the get-out-the-vote effort, invited me to join in on the lunch. I obliged, and not reluctantly. The food looked great.

There was fried chicken, greens, green beans, macaroni and cheese, and corn bread. I suspected that such a spread enticed church attendees to stick around after service for the get-out-the-vote event. Particularly striking at the church, more than anything, were the media outlets present. Although the church was small (less than 150 attendees), several media outlets, including PBS, CBS, and even one from the United Arab Emirates, were there to document what the church was doing in preparation for Souls to the Polls. The media's presence indicated the importance of Ohio in this election and the importance of the vote of black churchgoers.

Before heading to the polls, everyone was called to gather together in the church vestibule to consecrate the moment. The media gathered too, standing on the periphery of the crowd. This time, I felt a bit overdressed, wearing dress slacks and blouse with a dressy overcoat and heels. A thirty-something-looking woman, casually dressed in jeans, led congregants in a chant: "To the polls, to the polls . . . get your souls to the polls," to a gospel-like tune. The chant was repeated several times, accompanied by hand clapping. This scene seemed painfully forced, more a display for the media rather than a ritual that served the purpose of building unity and excitement. A reality of blackness, one that "the world" expected, was being performed. I struck up a casual conversation with a thirty-something black man in jeans, casual dress shirt, and blazer who happened to be standing next to me. He, like me, was more observing rather than participating in the singing. I surmised that he was not with the church. After striking up a chat, I learned that he was a director with what was then called PICO. He had flown out from California specifically for this event. The woman leading the singing was connected to PICO as well. What was particularly striking was that PICO was connected with a small, mainline Protestant black church and not any of the more prominent black churches in the city, which suggested a lack of access to the core of the black religious network in the city.

When the singing was done, an announcement was made that it was time to go to the polls. Vans were rented for people who preferred to go with the church. I drove my own car.

The traffic on the way to the county board of elections was heavy. Stop-and-go traffic extended at least two long blocks to the entrance of the voting site's parking lot. When I arrived, it was not easy finding a parking spot. I rode up and down the lanes for some time before I finally did. After I found a spot, I got out of my car and began taking in the scene. One person who stood out was Don Lemon, a news anchor with CNN. He popped out of a small passenger church bus with a TV crew in tow. Behind him, several African Americans got off the bus. I approached Lemon a little later to ask if he was aware of any media activities at other sites across the state. He confirmed what I guessed: CNN had television crews at election sites in major metro areas across Ohio.

There was a nervous excitement among the Obama volunteers; the electricity in the air (which was partly fueled by the near constant music booming from the OFA table situated at the back of the parking lot) reminded everyone present, especially the masses of likely Obama supporters standing in line—some for hours—that their cause was righteous. But in case they were unsure about the righteousness of their endeavors, the worship service that soon began let them know it was.

Only a small group of people, about twenty, gathered to watch the service. Nearly all were black, save for four twenty-something (or younger) white OFA campaign volunteers hanging around. Frankly, it did not matter that there were only twenty people watching the service because they were not the target audience. The audience was the thousands of people, African Americans especially, standing in the line to vote. The pastors and congregants who participated in the service aimed not only to invigorate President Obama's base—African American voters—but to imbue voting for President Obama with divine purpose. Together, they turned that parking lot into sacred ground.

The service began about two hours into early voting when a small cadre of people arrived and convened at the OFA campaign table. Everyone in the group was black. They were anywhere between about thirty and seventy years old. And they all wore Sunday-best clothing—suits, dress shoes, dresses, skirts, high heels, and dressy winter overcoats. Given the time of day they arrived, I presumed that they were coming directly from church.[4] A gentleman in the group set up a keyboard next to the OFA campaign table and connected it to the campaign's sound system. Once set up, he began to play. That was the cue for the rest of the group, which stood right in the middle of a driving lane directly in front of the OFA campaign table, to begin singing. Make no mistake about it: they owned that driving lane as they clapped, bobbed to the beat of the music, stomped their feet, played tambourines, and sang traditional gospel songs, their voices amplified by microphones.

And then there was the mime act performed by about fifteen middle and high schoolers, both girls and boys. The miming was a powerful act of artistic mobilization. Here we were at a department store turned into the county board of elections building. People were standing in a line so long that it extended out of the building, wrapped alongside it, and then turned the corner in on itself to form a pinwheel. The parking lot was packed. Drivers were inching along in the driving lanes in search of a spot. Amid all this were black teens dispersed throughout the parking lot in the driving lanes and between parked cars. Blaring from the speakers of the OFA sound system at the back of the parking lot was a Kirk Franklin song. The teens, facing the county board of elections building, moved in deliberate motion to the rhythm of the music with near expressionless faces, artfully incorporating sign language into the routine. Excluding their white gloves, they were dressed all in black. Their faces were painted in mime makeup: white with black accents around the lips and eyes.

Particularly striking about the scene was the teens' negotiation of a bright white six-inch-wide line painted on the ground of the parking lot one hundred feet from the entrance of the building. The line announced the boundary between legal and lawless campaigning. Ohio law prohibited any campaigning or electioneering within one hundred feet of an election site entrance (Ohio Legislature, n.d.). The youth were apparently aware of the meaning of this white line. Several of them stood right at the very edge of it, and some even had their toes just touching but never crossing the line, as they performed their act. Just a few feet away from those who were at the line was a tall, white, male uniformed police officer. The officer was surely there to make sure no one crossed that bright-white line. He stood there looking past the performance going on just feet away from him, all the while maintaining a rather indifferent countenance on his face.

The presence of youth meant that this was not an effort of just middle-aged or older people. Reminiscent of the civil rights movement, the get-out-the-vote effort in Ohio was multigenerational, including people from their teens to their eighties. We cannot know if doing a mime in the parking lot of the county board of elections was the youths' idea or that of adults in their church. Either way, they were there. And their presence was palpable. Their act was a not-so-subtle act of defiance of the government, teetering right at the edge of legal consequence.

After the youth were done miming, they returned to the OFA table. Soon after, two pastors arrived on the scene. One was Jackson Smith. Smith headed a large African American congregation in the city. Several other black religious leaders in this study mentioned him as one of the most influential pastors in the state. The other leader was Dexter Riley. Riley was relatively young, compared to other pastors in the study. He held a regional leadership position in one of the historically black denominations and had the reputation of being one of the most activist pastors in the city among his peers. Both men were dressed sharply in quite similar outfits: three-quarter-length dress overcoats, dress slacks, and dress shoes. And both had a charismatic air about them. They easily and confidently interacted with people hanging around the OFA campaign table. They laughed quite a bit during their conversations. Their interactions were easy. My sense was that Smith especially was a person in demand, this based on nothing more than how people interacted with him. He did not have to pursue people. They wanted to speak with him.

After networking a bit, Smith was given the mic. Upon doing so, he deliberately turned his body to face the county board of elections building. With that, he began to pray. His voice was booming and strong. When he spoke, one wanted to pay attention. Still, at the same time, he had an easy, bright smile and approachable demeanor. Similar to the youth performing the mime act, Smith too had to walk the line dividing legal and lawless political activity, as he negotiated separation of church and state in his prayer. His prayer was a thinly veiled attempt at bipartisanship as he asked for God's providence over the electoral process and guidance and protection for the president. Considering that he was right in front of the OFA campaign table and using the microphone connected to the campaign's sound system, it seems reasonable to assume that he hoped God would make sure President Obama was reelected.

Soon after Smith finished his prayer and left, the youth choir from Riley's church sang a few gospel songs. The program ended with them.

The parking-lot church service encouraged voters to stay the course, to not grow weary in well-doing. And they did not. Black voters, across the state, stood in line for hours to vote on that dreary fall Souls to the Polls Sunday.

When Opportunity Knocks

Broader social contexts matter for mobilization (McAdam 1982; Tilly 1978; Tarrow 1994; Cress and Snow 2000; Van Dyke 2003). Leaders have to recognize and understand the broader social context that they find themselves in because factors outside of their immediate spheres of influence constrain the goals they can pursue, making certain goals more achievable than others during certain time periods. These moments, what mobilization scholars call "political opportunities," matter not only for the emergence of social movements but also for the likelihood of their success (Kitschelt 1986; Meyer and Minkoff 2004).[5] Consequently, it is incumbent upon leaders to leverage events occurring in the political realm in such a way as to facilitate the likelihood of effective mobilization.

Mobilization of the black vote was going to be an uphill battle during Obama's second bid for the White House. As already noted, blacks were not as excited about Obama running up to the 2012 election as they were in 2008. Democrats were just off a major defeat in the 2010 elections. The political pendulum had swung far to the right, resulting in Republicans taking over the US House and nearly the Senate. But Republican attempts to sustain their momentum by restricting the capacity of Democratic voters, and African American voters especially in Ohio, turned out to be a major misstep. By acting the way they did when they did, Ohio Republicans created the right moment for black religious leaders in the state to mobilize. What this move did was give black religious leaders the necessary ingredient to mobilize the vote. When Ohio Republicans took aim at early voting, they positioned their actions to be framed as a threat to African Americans. Threats to a group are one of the primary motivators for social mobilization (Van Dyke 2003; Van Dyke and Soule 2002). Ohio black religious leaders recognized and seized on this to generate a frame that resonated with them as carriers of the civil rights movement legacy and with other African American Christians. And it worked.

The more important question, however, is why did this frame work? The civil rights movement took place more than fifty years prior. The movement led to tremendously important changes in the lives of blacks, particularly those in the South. Jim Crow segregation was dismantled. Barriers to voting had been minimized. The seeds for affirmative action had been planted. We saw opportunities for blacks open up, particularly so for those who were poised to take advantage of them (see Wilson 1978 for more). But much has happened since the 1960s and '70s. Loïc Wacquant (2014) argues that the changes in federal policies over the 1980s and '90s led to hyperincarceration and hyperghettoization.[6] The Reagan era created a system of hyperincarceration of black men on a scale never seen before. Temporary Assistance to Needy Families, signed into law by President Clinton, replaced Aid to Families with Dependent Children and eviscerated federal financial assistance to the poor and precipitated hyperghettoization. These two phenomena—hyperincarceration and hyperghettoization—Wacquant says, "are the two sides of the same historical coin. . . . Just as racial stigma was pivotal to the junction of hyperghetto and prison, the taint of blackness was central to the restrictive and punitive overhaul of social welfare. . . . Race turns out to be the symbolic linchpin that coordinated the synergistic transformation of these two sectors of public policy toward the poor" (2014, 45).[7] All this cumulative disadvantage regularly disrupts and diminishes the lives and life chances of blacks in the United States, poor blacks especially, and is occurring at a moment when racial language has been removed from laws and policies.

Herein lies the problem with how black religious leaders motivated mobilization; it depended on the ability to directly tie negative social outcomes to the legacy of the civil rights movement era. The frames of the civil rights movement era were generated to disassemble explicitly racist systems. The attempts of Ohio Republicans to minimize voting opportunities were not explicitly racial. Black religious leaders in the state nevertheless evoked in the collective memory the racial oppression and struggle that those who came before them endured as they fought for the freedom to vote. In a very real sense, as the struggle for freedom is central to the African American experience, the actions of Ohio Republicans were threatening what it meant to be African American.

Moreover, by aiming to undo a victory of the civil rights movement, access to the vote, they were threatening the legacy of the civil rights movement pastor as well. Therein lies a subtle inherent flaw in the frame that Ohio black religious leaders deployed to mobilize the black vote. At its core, the frame, while effective, was about protecting the legacy of the civil rights movement, not about undoing modern-day racist structures or discrimination.

A year after Obama was reelected, the US Supreme Court dealt a mighty blow to the Voting Rights Act, making access to the vote more vulnerable, especially so in the southern states. In other states, outside the South, other tactics have been used. Husted and Republicans continue to try to erect barriers to the vote in Ohio (ACLU Ohio, n.d.).[8] While they have had success with other law proposals, their attempts at minimizing Souls to the Polls have been challenged and have not, as of yet, led to systemic change to this tradition.[9] Still, the energy surrounding getting out the vote in Ohio in 2012 has not been duplicated since then. No sustained mobilization effort by black religious leaders in the state about anything, for that matter, has been discernable.

2

The Obama Effect

The election of Barack Obama as the forty-fourth president of the United States was an extraordinary historical development. The meaning of Barack Obama's presidency for race relations in the United States has been analyzed and debated in both scholarly and popular venues. This chapter addresses this topic as well, but through the reflections of black religious leaders. Our interviews capture the views of black religious leaders at a very particular moment in history. The first black president was in office, and the specter of Donald Trump's presidential campaign had not yet emerged. Black religious leaders expressed optimism but were also concerned about the depth of racism they encountered in society and from their fellow faith leaders. The pastors we interviewed were well positioned to understand the limits of what President Obama meant for race in the United States. Many of our interviewees' words seem prescient with the benefit of hindsight. While reelecting President Barack Obama was not as motivating for blacks in 2012 as it was for them in 2008, it did have particular meaning for many of the pastors in this study. We explore their thoughts on the Obama presidency (1) to inform how they think about race and racial identity in the United States and (2) to understand why they may choose to collectively mobilize.

For starters, it is important to note that the black pastors' perspectives on race in the United States were rooted in their standpoint. Every person's perspective is deeply influenced by their identities and experiences, particularly with regard to how one is situated in relation to power and privilege (P. Collins 1986, 2006; Harding 1993; Hartsock 1983). This is what is meant by "standpoint." In the United States, black religious leaders inhabit a unique standpoint. On the one hand, they are empowered community leaders who enjoy prestige and political influence. On the other hand, they are members of a subordinate group who experience racism and discrimination and head communities of color that experience the same. The perspectives of black religious leaders in this study are, in retrospect, prophetic. They discerned the signs of white supremacy evident at a moment when many people were proclaiming the United States to be a postracial society—a claim that is now clear to most astute people to be premature. Their prophetic voice is due to their particular standpoint.

In addition, the black religious leaders in this study identified with President Obama on multiple dimensions: race, gender, and position as leader. He was "them" in many ways, a highly educated prominent black man, a family man married to a black woman with black children. One could say that President Obama was an exemplar of the African American man. The pastors' admiration of President Obama was not just evident in what they said. It was also evident in some of their church décor. Commonly, we saw multiple professional-looking photographs of President Barack Obama and his family—at least eight by ten inches in size, although often much larger—prominently displayed in the offices or meeting rooms of black religious leaders in the study. Needless to say, they were very supportive of President Obama.

However, their support of President Obama was tainted with trepidation as they closely watched how the country was reacting to his leadership. In some way, perhaps, they looked carefully because President Obama's level of success would signal to them their potential success, their options. Could a black man truly be accepted as the leader of the United States of America, a white-supremacist society from its inception? Many pastors in our study were skeptical. In their view, the responses to the first black president, whether of certain Republican politicians or of some everyday whites, as represented by Tea Partiers, were blatant racism. While pundits in 2012 spoke of the Obama presidency as heralding a "postracial" future, the black religious leaders in this study rejected such a notion. It is obvious now that it was premature for commentators to make such a declaration. For many people, it was always a rather radical claim. How could one black person's "success" undo the institutional racism that permeated every corner of US society?

Barring a few examples, black religious leaders had high esteem for President Obama. And undergirding their views was the necessity for blacks to support one another, to not speak strongly against one of their own. African Americans, particularly in leadership positions, are often subjected to intense criticism that stems from racism rather than an objective assessment of leadership capabilities and accomplishments. For our interviewees, there was therefore a sense of being "in this together" with President Obama, whose experiences with racism reflected theirs.

President Obama's Leadership

The Symbolic Value of the Obama Presidency

The historic significance of the United States electing its first black president was not lost on black religious leaders. Wyoming Brashear, for instance, a very influential pastor whom you will learn more about in subsequent chapters, spoke poetically about this:

> When that announcement came across the screen, I saw the collective prayers of all of our ancestors, from 1619, and all of the bloodshed, the lynching, the sufferings, the jailing, the beatings, the broken hearts, and deferred dreams came together in that announcement. . . . It really was almost four hundred years of a process unfolding. . . . And, as Dr. King said in Memphis, "I have looked over, and I've seen the Promised Land. I may not get there with you; but, we, as a people, will get to the Promised Land." That's the kind of faith that carried President Obama in 2008.

For Brashear, seeing the announcement that Barack Obama won the US presidency was not simply a moment about validating Barack Obama as an individual. It was a victory for all black people across US history, even those who did not live to see it happen. It was a familiar narrative that he tells about race in the United States, one of black Americans' resistance through generations of pain and oppression to ultimately claim their rightful place as citizens and leaders. Barack Obama ascending to the highest office in the country was, in this framing, the culmination of hundreds of years of black struggle.

Another prominent black religious leader, Henry Taylor, also assigned special significance to the 2008 presidential election, particularly for the pride that blacks can feel knowing that a member of their race was selected as the "leader of the free world." This achievement was especially poignant because many black people thought that impossible. He said,

My father, when he died . . . he never thought that there could be a black president. He never dreamed it. And the fact that it happened . . . I think it was a sense of pride for me to say that in America, an African American can be president of the United States. But it wasn't just the fact that he was African American. It was the fact that he had ideas. He had a vision for the country. . . . That gave me a sense of sayin', "Yeah, we can vote for him, and we won't be ashamed."

The last statement in this quote is interesting and points to the perception of risk when supporting a black leader. This is not often discussed openly in mixed company, but for people of color, it can be nerve-wracking to see a person who looks like you in a high-stakes situation in which they will be judged on their performance. People of color are never seen as unmarked individuals the way white people are, and it is difficult to grow up in a racialized society without becoming very aware of what "they" say about "us" (Fanon 1967). Representation can feel risky and fragile because the missteps of an individual person of color can reflect poorly on their entire race. But for Taylor, Barack Obama inspired confidence and pride with his leadership style and widely appealing "vision for the country." Another pastor, Herman Murphy in Cincinnati, stated this same idea more directly: "My hope is that he will dispel the rumor that African Americans can't lead."

Black religious leaders were also acutely aware of President Obama's potential impact on the future of the black experience in the United States. Brian McCormick reflected on the 2008 election by saying, "[It was] very powerful. . . . It gave a sense of pride for many of the African American youth. . . . They never thought they would see an African American as president. . . . So, they'll say, 'Now, I can be the president.' So, yeah, it gave a sense of hope." For this pastor, the "sense of hope" generated by Obama's election created a new set of possibilities for black youth. McCormick believed that with Barack Obama as president, black kids could grow up with a different and more empowering set of expectations. This general point was echoed by several pastors in our sample. McCormick continued, "You know, back years ago, you'd say, 'Well, yeah. You can be president.' You know, but you kind of in the back of your mind, 'Yeah, it probably isn't going to happen.' . . . But now you can say, 'Yeah, you can be president.' To me that's such a positive. That black kids and white kids can see that a black man can be a president." These quotes show that, for these pastors, Barack Obama was a symbol that they could deploy to inspire and empower the youth in their communities. Instead of the message "It will never happen" that previous generations received, post-Obama youth would know a world where a black man could rise to the most exalted position at that time in US society.

Several pastors noted that Barack Obama's presidency was important because of how he embodied and displayed black excellence in a way that was in line with the conservative, Christian family values promoted by the black church. Tyrone Coleman articulated this when he said, "The president doesn't have to say a doggone thing about the black family. When he walked out on that stage election night, that said it all. Every time you see him getting off Air Force One, with Sasha and Malia, or every time you see him with the First Lady, . . . he doesn't have to say it. He is it!" Coleman observed that Barack Obama, by virtue of being president while black, could make strong racialized statements through his actions. He could model what was possible for black families just by being visible and loving his family in public. In a country where positive representations of black families are rare and outweighed by a strong focus on crime and dysfunction in black communities, the image of Barack Obama as a strong leader and family man was an important symbolic resource.

Leaders of all stripes face similar dilemmas, like how to inspire people, motivate them, and bring them together across difference. Black leaders face the added obstacle of racism. It is clear that the black religious leaders we interviewed identified strongly with President Obama. Some pastors explicitly pointed to President Obama as a model for their own leadership. Jason Armstrong from Cincinnati explained, "Barack does the right things for the right reason. . . . That said something to me, that as a pastor, you know, can I do things for the right reasons—not political, not biased, but in my role, being fair, whether it's a member that I'm close to or a member that I just met. . . . So I learned that from seeing somebody like him." Armstrong took cues from President Obama and attempted to emulate his leadership style. In his interview, he cited specific examples from Obama's time in office, including how Obama remained calm and collected in the face of people calling him a liar during a State of the Union Address. Armstrong paralleled that example with his own experiences with congregants questioning his leadership, saying, "Because we could be in the church, and somebody [yells], 'Pastor, that ain't true!" and I'd be wanting to say, 'Hey, it is!' . . . So I learned that from him. . . . Just keep your cool. Don't say anything." This pastor admired President Obama's response to the difficult conditions he faced and saw this incident as providing relevant lessons for his own pastoral leadership. President Obama was a role model in a literal sense: a fellow black leader who faced similar obstacles, solved similar problems, and, in Armstrong's estimation, did so with poise and moral integrity.

As previously stated, black religious leaders identified with President Obama on multiple levels. This identification showed up clearly in the interviews, with leaders seeing his victory as a historic achievement in the face of a shared burden of racism. They saw his example as a hopeful symbol for black children and even an exemplary model for black leaders like themselves who aimed to lead with integrity in their families, communities, and churches.

"Cut the Brother a Break": Reviews of the Obama Presidency

One question posed to all interviewees was, "What do you think about the idea that President Obama hasn't done enough for African Americans?" This idea was common in the political discourse of the time. Pundits wondered whether his relative silence on the issue of race would hurt his image in the black community. And indeed, one might expect black leaders to advocate for race issues to be front and center in Obama's presidency. However, our interviews indicate that black religious leaders were far more concerned with economic issues. Religious leaders expressed varying degrees of satisfaction with what Obama had accomplished in his first term, but for the most part, reviews of Obama's first term were positive. Many expressed sympathy with the difficulty of being a black leader in a racist society and framed Obama's first term as a success for black people, while also (often reluctantly) acknowledging areas of disagreement and areas where he had come up short from their perspective.

When asked about what President Obama had done for black Americans, Reginald Baker in Cincinnati did not mince words:

> You don't have to put Kente cloth or dashikis on everything in order for it to be black. . . . Blacks need jobs. Blacks need health care. . . . I think

the president has done a good job of being the president of the country, and I think blacks have been able to benefit from that, specifically his passions with economics, education, and health care. If that's not on the black agenda, I don't know what in the world would be on the black agenda.

Baker downplayed the suggestion that Obama had not done enough for African Americans and instead talked about how he had been a good leader and helped all Americans. He emphasized how black people had benefited from his victories on economic issues. Conrad Stevenson made a similar point: "Well, black people get sick. He got health care. . . . Black people have houses. Well, [he] turned the foreclosure thing around. Black people drive cars. Well, he kept the car industry going. I mean, he's done a lot for black people. He's done a lot for the whole nation." This was a common theme. The pastors whom we interviewed, for the most part, did not want Barack Obama to talk about race more or amp up his performative blackness. They instead emphasized President Obama's work on other matters, such as passing health care reform and turning the economy around after the recession. While having a black president was meaningful to these pastors, it was also clear that they were evaluating his leadership on a more universal basis, not just in relation to what he did for black people. Black religious leaders articulated a vision for Barack Obama's leadership that went beyond what he meant for black American representation and instead focused on how he was a leader for all Americans.

Perhaps, in part, because of black religious leaders' identification with President Obama, there was a marked reluctance to criticize him. This is exemplified by Timothy Matson, who said, "I'm not going to Monday-morning-quarterback the president." In another revealing example, Herman Wilson stated, "I don't particularly like the posture that some of *our critics—or his critics*—have taken. Because I think he's an intelligent man, and I respect him as president. . . . I also know that he is more than just president for African Americans. . . . I trust that he's going to make good decisions that's going to impact everybody" (emphasis added). Wilson emphasized the trust and respect that he saw as President Obama's due. There was a sense that when he was talking about President Obama, he was also speaking about black leaders more broadly. To criticize President Obama was to criticize black men's leadership in general. In the interviews, it was important for Wilson and many others to frame Obama as not only a leader for black people but also a leader for all, one who deserved respect, even trust.

This narrative of universal leadership was also present in discussions about the one issue about which pastors diverged from the president: his stance toward homosexuality and gay marriage. Several pastors made it plain that they disagreed with the president on this issue. A few others chose to defer. However, only one pastor said that he did not vote for Obama because of this issue. For all others, their identification with Obama and agreement about economic issues overshadowed their disagreement on homosexuality.[1]

Interestingly, many pastors' statements about this topic seemed like they were already thought out, prepared, even rehearsed. Here is a selection of representative quotes:

> As a politician, you have to be a politician for everybody in your community, and there's gay people in the community. I got that. . . . He's not the pastor of the country; he's the president of the country. . . . At the end of the day, who sleeps with who is not as important as, "Can you get these brothers out here some jobs?"

> Like, Obama, to me, is not the pastor of the United States. He's the president, and he has to be the president of everyone.

> I would say this, we did not elect a pope. We elected a president. . . . While I don't agree with his position on it, I understand it. Because there's three hundred million people in this country, and diversity is good for the country.

While pastors disagreed with gay marriage on religious grounds, they did not argue that their religious objection should be encoded in law. The line that Obama was "not the pastor of the country; he's the president of the country" was a common way for pastors across the state to frame the issue. Ultimately, for the vast majority of the religious leaders in our sample, the issue of gay marriage was secondary to the economy and the historic nature of Barack Obama's presidency.

The interviews indicate that this overlap in messaging was not accidental. One pastor in our sample, Stephen Foster, was an outlier in that he was very critical of President Obama, in particular of his lack of attention to black issues and representation. He expressed frustration with the mandates levied by other black religious leaders:

> What we're basically being told is to "shut up" and "don't criticize Obama." And that's what we're being told. And, "Don't say anything about the same-sex marriages. Don't say that. He's the first black president." . . . Leadership has a way of not entertaining the subject [criticizing Obama]. And, when it's brought up, they'll say, "Well, we're going to put that on the next agenda," but you will never see. Well, you know, Stevie Wonder can see that they don't want to talk about this, and so it never comes back up.

When Foster expressed disapproval of President Obama to other black religious leaders, they responded by emphasizing the importance of not criticizing the first black president. In meetings of the local pastoral association, the leaders, according to him, stonewalled attempts to address the issue openly. The narrative about the separation between politics and religious morality was promoted, and leadership communicated a clear message: support President Obama. Foster's account just quoted was corroborated by Jackson Smith:

> I told some preachers—back after he first got elected, and they were talking that stuff—I said, "Look. Okay. Here's the bottom line. He's not coming to your family reunion, and he's not coming to Big Mama's funeral. Okay? Now, stop it." . . . "Just because he's black, he's not coming to everything we have." . . . But you've got to give the brother a little break. He's the first one. And he has all the forces against him. The fact he's gotten anything done is nothing short of miraculous. They met the night of the inauguration, while he was dancing with his wife. They met to decide, "How can we make him a one-term president?" They were never going to give him a chance. Cut the brother a break.

For Smith, it was important for black religious leaders not to judge President Obama harshly for not attending events hosted by black organizations. In his view, black religious leaders should "cut the brother a break" and not be vocal critics of the administration. Instead, they should emphasize Obama's accomplishments in the face of strong and committed, often racist, opposition. As fellow members of a marginalized racial group, black leaders should not criticize one of their own.

Thus, the Ohio black religious leaders we interviewed gave President Obama's first term very positive reviews overall. They were primarily concerned about the economy, jobs, and health care, and these issues took precedence over their disagreement with him on the issue of gay marriage. There was social pressure to emphasize Obama's accomplishments, downplay criticisms of him, and acknowledge the difficult context that he dealt with. Implicit in these interviews is a recognition that the public discourse about Obama's leadership and accomplishments had implications for how they, themselves, were able to be recognized as legitimate and effective leaders by wider society. Unfortunately, what they saw in society's reaction to Barack Obama's presidency was not always hopeful.

President Obama's Impact on US Race Relations

While many pastors in our sample viewed Barack Obama's presidency as a historic achievement for blacks and a hopeful sign for race relations in the United States, they were also acutely aware of and apprehensive about the racist backlash. Like Obama, black religious leaders were also visible leaders in a country that devalues the intellect, intentions, and actions of black people. Many of their observations about societal responses to the Obama presidency are astute and prescient, especially when considered in light of Donald Trump winning the US presidency despite using blatantly racist language while campaigning in 2016.

"Racism Is Still Alive and Well": A Sobering Assessment

Some of our interviews took place in the months after Obama won the 2012 election. Several pastors viewed Obama's second term as a reason for optimism and hope about race relations in the United States. One pastor explained, "I was very proud of America when they voted him back in, because, as I said earlier, black and Hispanic people couldn't have been the only ones. We had to come together as a nation that we're going to give him another chance, and that was deliberate. . . . We have a long way to go, but we're on our way." While one win could be portrayed as luck or a fluke, perhaps due to the 2008 financial meltdown, Obama winning the presidency twice meant that the country validated his bid for continued leadership. One significant aspect of this, as noted, was that many white people had to support Obama's bid for a second term. This pastor viewed this support as significant and a reason for pride in the country. His assertion that "we're on our way" framed Obama's presidency as a sign of progress in US race relations.

However, most pastors did not express such a rosy view. For them, rather than being a sign of racial progress, Barack Obama's presidency uncovered the depths of racism in US society. Ernest Conway described how his initial optimism gave way to a sober realization that racism was still strong:

> [In 2008] I really thought for about ten days that [the election of Barack Obama] marked a major shift in this country. And it did, except that it exposed some things that we thought had been settled. And we discovered that it not only had not been settled, it had become hardened and . . . and desperate. . . . Everybody's got a different view of what they mean by "racism." But I mean the hatred and the absolute willingness to sacrifice everything on behalf of that hate—and no desire anymore to even cover it up. If everybody thinks that that's just about Barack Obama, they're sadly mistaken.

Conway argued that Obama's presidency "exposed" the reality of racism in United States: that there are many people whose racial hatred overrode reason, even self-interest. For certain segments of society, the emergence of a popular black leader was the catalyst for open expressions of hatred. To declare open, explicit racism dead was quite hasty. Thus, while many Americans in 2012 believed that Obama's presidency was a clear sign of an inevitable postracial future, Conway's perspective seems, in hindsight, to be closer to the truth.

Black religious leaders' solidarity with Barack Obama was tied to their awareness of how racism is a serious (and often seriously unfair) obstacle to his leadership. They took note when Obama was not afforded the same respect shown to white politicians. One bishop, Edward

Quincy, said, "You can hear racism on the television, on the radio. . . . I heard somebody call the president a 'liar.' They'd want to electrocute you, if you called another president a liar. The disrespect that they outwardly show—no respect at all. If he was white, they wouldn't do that." While calling President Obama a "liar" is not an explicitly racialized slur, Quincy attributed this outburst to racism, noting that the behavior deviated from the deference and respect shown to previous (white) presidents. He also pointed out how racism was transmitted through the media. Another pastor, Bill Brown, echoed these ideas: "I think if white America and black America would be honest what the last two elections showed, specifically this one, is that racism is still alive and well. Just the disrespect shown to President Obama by professional politicians to me was just unreal." Far from seeing Obama's presidency as an indicator of an emerging "postracial" consensus, many black religious leaders' takeaway from how he was treated while in office was that racism in the United States was "still alive and well."

Similarly, Joseph Butler observed that not only did President Obama deal with significant disrespect and distrust from both political and media figures but his accomplishments were also undercelebrated:

> Nothing is really celebrated. All the jobs that we lost have been regained. That's a fact. You know? We have Obamacare. That's a fact. You know? He has scaled down the wars. That's a fact. . . . None of those things have been celebrated. . . . Had that been a white man, every one of 'em would have been celebrated. . . . And you have the leader of the Republican Party say on national TV that his only concern was that Barack Obama have a four-year presidency, . . . one term.

By and large, the pastors in this study were very in tune to the way President Obama was consistently undermined. They noticed and articulated the mechanisms by which his leadership was blocked, his influence diminished, and his accomplishments downplayed. This makes sense given their standpoint: those who experience racism themselves are intimately acquainted with how it undermines a person's power and influence.

Another common theme in our interviews was exasperation at the numerous seemingly petty and illogical objections to President Obama's leadership. These objections were perceived as obstacles erected simply to hinder President Obama. They had nothing to do with what he was doing but were more about who he was. These objections took on a broader meaning for black religious leaders than just hindering Obama's presidency and political goals. Dexter Riley said,

> I feel that if Obama went out and looked up in the sky and said that it was blue, that he could not have gotten everyone in the Senate and the House of Representatives to say, "Yes, the sky is blue." . . . Me as an African American male, I think a lot of that was racism, racist, that I think that some people were determined that he would not have a successful term. . . . I think it says to the rest of us in America that race still matters. . . . I usually don't do the race thing. I mean, I'm one of those persons that tries to be very open, very objective. Don't do the race thing. But I think a lot of this was about race.

Riley argued that President Obama faced significant, even ridiculous, obstacles because of racism. He noted that his perspective as a black man influenced his view but tempered this by assuring the interviewer that he usually did not "do the race thing." For Riley, the people putting obstacles in front of President Obama were broadcasting a message to the nation that a black man as leader cannot and will not stand. The reality was that whether a black man could lead effectively in the United States was not only up to President Obama. It was apparent that powerful forces were constantly working to hinder any person of color from achieving what they set out to do, even if it was to the benefit of all.

In fact, one of the most revealing outcomes of the Obama presidency was to show just how invested racist white people are in whiteness. Their anger and obstinance run deep. For many of the pastors in this study, the sheer hysteria that greeted President Obama's rather-moderate proposals for reform exposed the true face of white supremacy. Conrad Stevenson described this unmasking, so to speak, of certain segments of the United States:

> But even just having him in the White House to me just changes the atmosphere of the nation. . . . I was teasing somebody. I said, "You know, growing up, we used to think that white people were pretty sharp. You

know, if you're white, you're right," and all that kind of stuff. I said, "Now, through this last election, white people are showing they just as ignorant as anybody else." Because the stuff that they were upset about Obama for just didn't even make sense.

White supremacy is a system that rests on the belief that whites are intellectually and morally superior to and consequently more worthy of power and dominance than people of color. President Barack Obama was a revealing foil because, whether or not one agrees with his politics, he exemplified what was normatively constructed as "excellence" on many fronts. From his calm demeanor, strong speaking skills, ethical record, and lofty ideals to his affection for and commitment to his family and Christian faith, Obama embodied many of the qualities that most Americans, particularly those who are white, middle class, and Christian, admire. The juxtaposition of a demonstrably intelligent and widely admired black man with the often vitriolic attacks launched at him by whites made it difficult to maintain the fiction that white people are better off because they are superior to people of color. It was much harder to believe that "white is right" under such circumstances.

One pastor argued that the political class needed to pay more heed to race relations in the United States. After describing how the Obama presidency revealed cleavages in US society, Tyrone Thomas from Cleveland said,

> We need to be equally serious about race relations. . . . They've analyzed this election process inside out, upside down and have been very creative to have a poll every day that's different from the poll the day before. . . . So if you can be that analytical about that, you can also be so analytical about our relationship and how—how we can move towards fixing it, . . . ["we" meaning] black America and white America.

In 2012, in the wake of Obama's first term, it was clear to Thomas that the political class needed to pay more attention to race. Unfortunately, the Democratic Party and affiliated politicos did not listen to the voices of people like Thomas. In the postmortem of the 2016 election, pundits and political experts struggled to explain the results. Steve Phillips, in

Brown Is the New White (2016), convincingly argues that the Democratic Party's fatal error was overreliance on upwardly mobile white men, noting that over 97 percent of campaign funds spent on consulting in 2014 went to white-owned firms. This means that white people overwhelmingly designed the political strategy of the Democratic Party, including the polls Thomas discussed. Many of those white people thought that Obama's presidency meant that race was less of a factor than it had been previously. This blind spot cost the Democratic Party dearly in 2016.

"White Trumps Faith": Observations about White Evangelicals

One of the "surprises" of the 2016 election was the strong support that Donald Trump received from white evangelical leaders and churches. The Pew Research Center reported that 81 percent of white evangelicals voted for Trump in 2016, a greater percentage than votes reportedly cast for Bush and Romney (Martinez and Smith 2016). Nearly four years later, their support of him remains nearly as strong (Lipka and Smith 2020). But this would come as no surprise to black religious leaders. In this section, we show that in 2012 many of them were painfully aware of what was going on in white evangelical circles well before 2016.

Black religious leaders' standpoint includes not only their race and gender but also their role as pastors. Black Protestants tend to be theologically conservative, similar to white evangelicals. This facilitated a particular awareness by black pastors of how their white colleagues were responding to President Obama. Several pastors questioned white evangelicals' religious grounds for opposition to Barack Obama and embrace of the Republican candidate, Mitt Romney. Butler stated,

> So I know a lot of white evangelicals support [Mitt Romney]. Why do you think that is? [*Laughs*] Because they can't take a black man being president. You know? It's amazing to me that all these evangelicals—President Obama was running—they said he was the anti-Christ. The world was coming to an end. Oh, they did everything. Now Romney is of the Mormon faith, . . . not the Christian faith, the Mormon faith, who is against all that Christians believe. Not a one of them has come out against Romney. . . . How is it that Romney can be so right and Obama was so wrong?

Butler argued that white evangelicals' intense opposition to Obama, including insinuations that he was the antichrist (which is akin to calling him the devil incarnate), stemmed from their not wanting a black man to be president. Like many other conservative Christians, he identified Mormonism as a separate religion and did not consider it Christian. So in his view, white evangelicals' support for Mitt Romney was not due to religious similarity but rather to racial similarity.

One pastor, Derek Brown, had some particularly poignant words about his white evangelical colleagues:

> When Romney announced he was going to run, the white Christians, those right-wingers, evangelicals had a fit. "Mormonism is a cult. Mormonism is a cult. Mormonism is a cult." But the closer he got to the nomination, you didn't hear it. They start accepting it because white trumps faith. . . . The closer [Romney] got to the nomination, they started drawing back. "Mormonism now is okay. It's okay to be a Mormon. Well, we don't think religion ought to come into it. . . . There is no religious test in America for presidency. . . ." Blah, blah, blah. Why? Because white trumps faith! They would rather die and go to hell.

In evangelicals' rhetorical pivot on Romney, Brown saw clear evidence that the animating mechanism of white evangelicals' Republican political affiliation was race, not religion. As he so plainly put it, "White trumps faith."

These pastors' comments are particularly prescient given what happened soon thereafter. In the waning days of President Obama's second term, Donald Trump ran an openly racist presidential campaign and found a very robust base of support among white evangelicals. Many people pointed out that Donald Trump was an odd choice to be the face of Christian values, with his storied sexual history, seeming indifference to their primary issue of abortion, and demeaning attacks on women. However, historians have noted that the political activities of white evangelical churches have been motivated more by concerns about race than by abortion (Balmer 2014). Prominent white scholars of race and religion prior to 2016 emphasized that there was not strong evidence of racism in survey data of white evangelicals. Instead, they pointed to individualistic attitudes (Emerson and Smith 2000) or differences in moral views related to sex (Putnam and Campbell 2010) to explain white evangelicals' political behavior. There was not discussion of how these seemingly nonracial views and attitudes may be connected to racism; these researchers did not measure or account for the "colorblind" racism that emerged in the post-civil-rights context (Bonilla-Silva 2001).

After the 2016 election, research by white academics began to emerge showing how white evangelicals' racial views line up with white Christian nationalism (Gorski 2017; Tope et al. 2017; Whitehead, Perry, and Baker 2018). A PRRI/Brookings survey in fall 2016 found an interesting shift in white evangelicals' views. In 2011, only 30 percent said that "an elected official who commits an immoral act in their personal life can still behave ethically and fulfill their duties." In 2016, the percentage had increased to 72 percent (PRRI 2016). These results seem to indicate that white evangelicals' moral views were shifting to accommodate support for Donald Trump. Thus, research done by credentialed experts in the wake of Trump's successful candidacy supports what Brown said about white evangelicals in 2012.

* * *

This chapter has focused on several of the patterns we found in Ohio black religious leaders' opinions about Barack Obama's presidency and leadership. Pastors spoke about the symbolic importance of his presidency for black people. His ascendancy to this office served as a powerful role model to young people, black children especially. However, they were far less inclined to make any pronouncements about Obama's impact on race relations in the United States as a whole. They recognized the racist backlash for what it was: a powerful force guiding the attitudes and actions of a significant subset of white Americans, many of whom professed similar conservative Christian beliefs as they did.

Why would black religious leaders have special insight into the meaning of reactions to Barack Obama's presidency? The answer is their unique standpoint. One thing that comes through clearly in these interviews is that many of the pastors we spoke to were very aware of power: what it looks like, how it works, and how it can be undermined. Running a church requires considerable knowledge and skill and a keen awareness of how authority and the exercise of it works. Implicit in many pastors' incredulity about the disrespect shown to President Obama was a question: What does it say about black religious leaders' ability to exercise power and authority when a black man occupying the highest office of the land can be treated with such blatant disrespect? These pastors saw clearly that racism in the United States was alive and well in the midst of the Obama era, shaping white people's thinking and behavior, despite the fact that many white pundits and scholars were in denial about this fact.

It is important to note that in each case, whether it was supporting candidate Obama despite disagreement on gay marriage or not criticizing his economic policies, there were always dissenters, pastors who did not toe the party line. But those exceptions often served to highlight the rule: that there was significant social pressure to conform to the party line of supporting President Obama. Black religious leaders and white evangelical pastors are thus similar in more than just their theological conservatism. There are similarities between how many black religious leaders responded to Barack Obama and how we are observing many white evangelical pastors respond to Donald Trump. But, in our opinion, there is no moral equivalence between these cases. Pastors' responses cannot be detached from the broader white supremacist, patriarchal structure in which we all are embedded. To affirm a black man who, aside from his support of LGBTQ rights, exhibited many of the qualities that many Americans, regardless of race, Christian or otherwise, aspire toward is not morally equivalent to supporting a person who repeatedly makes explicitly and implicitly derogatory statements about the more disadvantaged people in society, including people of color (Graham et al. 2019), women (Walsh 2018), and those with disabilities (Arkin 2015). Black pastors were excited about someone who affirmed their humanity and worth as black male leaders in a world that routinely denies them that dignity. Even still, as was revealed in chapter 1, reelecting the first black president was not the catalyst for their mobilization in 2012. That too is an important distinction.

3

The Civil Rights Movement Credential

Black religious leaders in Ohio contributed to a historic black voter turnout in 2012. However, as far as the people in our study knew, black religious leaders in the state had not participated in any mobilization that went beyond the local level for any issue within recent years, except voter mobilization. But why? One reason, we suggest, has to do with how the black religious leader network worked. It was hierarchical and dense. Only certain leaders, who we call *principal leaders*, had the influence to initiate and then sustain broad mobilization efforts among fellow leaders. Principal leaders were the ones who got to decide if, when, and for what to mobilize. What distinguished a principal leader from other leaders is that they sat atop the hierarchy. A principal leader might occupy a formal position of leadership in their organization to which other leaders reported (e.g., bishop) or possessed sufficient influence within a network of leaders such that other leaders followed their direction—or both. Of course, other leaders in the network were influential. About 20 percent of the black religious leaders were what we consider high status, that is, religious leaders who were denominational bishops or had been identified by at least three other religious leaders in our study as being particularly influential. Still, the breadth of power of high-status leaders was limited compared to the principal leader. Principal leaders had influence over high-status leaders, who had power over other leaders, and so on.

Principal leaders were essential for mobilization that extended beyond the local level for two interrelated and equally important reasons. The first reason is they were needed to initiate mobilization. This step— the decision to act or not and, if so, when—is a critically important step for social mobilization.[1] The principal leader established what the goal of mobilization should be and when to work toward that goal, effectively setting mobilization efforts in motion. As we watched action develop among the black clergy we studied, it was at a principal leader's direction that other leaders in the network got other people within their realm of influence to act.

The second reason principal leaders were essential was that they, unlike other leaders, could get other leaders near and far, both socially (e.g., across organizations) and geographically (e.g., across the state), to engage in mobilization efforts aimed at achieving the same goal. What this means is that a certain leader or a few connected leaders who are not principal leaders may be able to initiate localized or intermittent mobilization efforts. They may also mobilize a small number of other leaders to perhaps protest against or lobby for local political or social action. There is repeated evidence in this study of religious leaders mobilizing other leaders to work toward a social or political outcome at the neighborhood level and sometimes at the city level. Some examples include organizing to get retail and grocery stores in their churches' neighborhoods, protesting racial discrimination in city-issued contracts, or organizing for racial equality in school funding. Principal leaders, on the other hand, generated social action beyond the local level.

The power of the principal leader, however, does not derive from their own prowess. It derives from certain characteristics embedded in the leader network. In the case of black religious leaders in this study, two characteristics in particular helped give certain people access to the status of principal leader. One is what we call the *civil rights movement credential*. A legitimate claim of some kind of connection to the civil rights movement is what gave a black religious leader civil rights movement credentials. The civil rights movement credential is rooted in black religious leaders' nostalgic reverence for the civil rights movement era, which is a deep respect and awe of the era, in particular its political and legislative outcomes and the black pastors who mobilized to achieve them. Black religious leaders with civil rights movement credentials were propelled to the top of the candidate list for principal leader. The other characteristic that gave the principal leader power is the informal, hierarchical structure of the black religious leader network. Obedience to those who were more highly esteemed in the black religious leader network was taken for granted and even expected, as our discussion about supporting Obama implied. This enabled pastors who had civil rights movement credentials to have considerable influence over their peers. When a principal leader made a decision or gave a directive, the informal hierarchical character of the black religious leader network ensured that a good deal of the black religious leaders within the principal leader's sphere of influence would follow. And it is then that broad mobilization could get under way. Without the hierarchical structure of the network, the breadth of influence of a person with civil rights movement credentials would be limited.

Charisma and the Principal Leader

For all intents and purposes, a principal leader is a charismatic leader.[2] This person may occupy a formal position of power, but their capacity to mobilize other leaders is rooted in their charismatic authority. Aldon Morris and Cedric Herring (1984) similarly recognized charisma as an important factor for social movement leadership, expanding on Max Weber's (1947, 1968) conceptualization of the concept.[3] They point out that Morris in his book *The Origins of the Civil Rights Movement* "found that in the civil rights movement charisma and organization were cojoined from the very beginning and were mutually reinforcing" (Morris and Herring 1984, 69). Our study similarly highlights the role of charisma.

While a good deal of research on charismatic authority emphasizes qualities particular to the person, more recent work emphasizes the role of groups for charisma (Hogg 2001; Lord, Brown, and Harvey, 2001; Haslam and Platow 2001; Hogg and Knippenberg 2003). Leaders are understood to be charismatic when they possess a quality or set of qualities that is cherished by their followers (Knippenberg 2011). Charisma is, therefore, not a quality that a person possesses but a power that a person's group confers to a person. This is a subtle yet critically important distinction. It means that principal leaders are actually beholden to the groups they lead.[4]

A charismatic leader gains influence because the person is perceived by their group as having not simply exemplary qualities but qualities that are thought to be representative of the group (Abram and Hogg 1990; Hogg and Turner 1987; Turner 1991). These are qualities that the group cherishes and understands to be most reflective of what it means to be a group member. These qualities might include certain values (e.g., justice), beliefs (e.g., Christian), and identities (e.g., marital status) or affiliations (e.g., political, recreational, clubs) as well as ways of presenting oneself in, say, speech or dress. It does not much matter what the quality or set of qualities is, so long as it is valued by the group. The reason a person in any group can emerge as a leader is because in all groups there is variation. Some group members have more of those qualities that the group says matter than others do. The person (or persons) who has enough (where "enough" is also determined by the group) of these qualities is seen as especially representative of who the group is or aspires to be, and they become an example of how group members should think, feel, and act. This gives these group members power over other group members, their behaviors, emotion, beliefs, and attitudes and facilitates these especially representative people's ascent to positions of leadership (Hogg and Knippenberg 2003; Knippenberg 2011; Knippenberg, Lossie, and Wilkie 1994). A principal leader, then, is a member of a group, network, or community of leaders who possesses a quality (or set of qualities) that the group cherishes, and because of this, other leaders in the group, network, or community see this person as someone worthy of emulating and following.

The Civil Rights Movement Credential

The particular quality that helped produce and sustain principal leaders among black pastors in our study was the civil rights movement credential. Black ministers who participated in the civil rights movement or who could claim some connection to the civil rights movement were bestowed the status of principal leaders and the power that goes with it. The civil rights movement credential mattered because black religious leaders in the study maintained a nostalgic reverence for the civil rights movement. This reverence was firmly rooted in a theology that says black Christianity is prophetic and priestly (Lincoln and Mamiya 1990).

Nearly all the black religious leaders in the sample, when asked what they believed to be the primary responsibilities of pastors, framed the role of the pastor in this way. Several actually used this specific language in their descriptions. One black religious leader explained it in these terms: "I believe that a pastor's role . . . is dualistic. . . . Not only did [Jesus] heal and preach and teach, but he also fought against the religious blocks of his day. And so to me, a pastor not only needs to be a pulpiteer—in the pulpit—but also one that's prophetic in the streets." Another presented a similar view:

> The primary responsibility of a pastor is—as I see it—to tend to their flock, to preach and teach the Gospel of Jesus Christ, and to provide pastoral care and counseling. . . . Secondarily, I see the role of the pastor to be a voice in the community, social justice, to also be a prophetic voice. And by "prophetic," I don't mean . . . foretelling, like a soothsayer, but prophetic by speaking truth to power.

With few exceptions, black religious leaders in the study said pastors were commissioned to be both preachers who took care of their congregants and leaders who were civically engaged, especially in issues salient to the black community. There can be little doubt that some of the most iconic examples of black religious leaders embodying these roles are those who were involved in the civil rights movement. As one respondent put it, "When you think of Martin Luther King, he was a religious leader first before he was a civil rights leader. He used his voice and his gift to share the dream that I believe was from God of how this country should respect each other as it relates to race, you know. And so the model of a religious leader having a voice of social justice I think is the best role." Another respondent referenced Jesse Jackson, also a black religious leader involved in the civil rights movement, saying, "I really believe the statement that . . . that great and notable civil rights figure Jesse Jackson made years ago: we may have come over here on different boats or different ships, but we're in the same boat now." Another considered "civil rights" to describe the agenda of the black interdenominational alliances in which he participated, saying, "Our ecumenical, interfaith discussions at the regional or national level, there is consistent dialogue and positions, in terms of being supportive of the civil rights / political rights movement." A thirty-something black religious leader referenced "civil rights" in a vision for younger black religious leaders' social activism, saying, "I think it's something else that the newer generation is doing now from civil rights: is not just teaching people to march is important but empowering people to know how to set up a march, . . . why we need a march."

Collectively, the way in which the civil rights movement in particular and civil rights generally were discussed revealed a high value placed on the legacy of the civil rights movement and the leaders who organized it. It further suggests why possessing civil rights movement credentials catapulted certain people to the status of principal leader. There are other characteristics that were valued. These included graduating from a historically black college or university (HBCU), being a man, and heading a congregation affiliated with a black denomination. But the civil rights movement credential was the quintessential quality of a black religious leader. It symbolized for the black religious leaders in this study who they were, or at least who they aspired to be, both prophets and priests. And it was the black religious leader community's nostalgic reverence for the civil rights movement era that gave this credential its value.

Who Were the Principal Leaders?

There were two people who clearly emerged as principal leaders in the Ohio black religious leader network: Wyoming Brashear and Mark Thompson. You were already introduced to Mark Thompson. The influence of Brashear and Thompson extended across religious boundaries. Black religious leaders from a variety of denominations and religious affiliations looked to them for direction and followed their lead.

Of the two, Wyoming Brashear most epitomized the principal leader for Ohio black religious leaders, largely because he actually participated in the civil rights movement and knew several key leaders of the movement personally. Other black religious leaders expressed tremendous respect for him. They followed his lead unquestioningly.

Take, for example, Jackson Smith's description of Brashear. You might recall that Smith was the pastor who prayed at the church service in the parking lot of the county board of elections in chapter 1. Smith shared that he got engaged in the 2012 get-out-to-vote efforts in the state because Brashear asked him to. For Smith, there was only one answer to Brashear's request. He explained, punctuating his comment with a hearty laugh, "A man like Brashear, . . . who's an icon—if Wyoming Brashear calls, nobody's going to tell him no. Nobody!" There are two key points in this brief but powerfully illustrative statement. One is that

Brashear is esteemed as an "icon," explicitly understood to be representative of black religious leaders. The second is Brashear's influence. All he needed to do was ask, and other leaders followed him. As Smith put it, "nobody's going to tell him no."

It is important to note that Smith was influential in his own right. Several other religious leaders in the study described him as such and mentioned that he was one of the more active leaders in their network when it came to civic activity. Additionally, while many respondents highlighted Brashear as an important figure in the black religious leader community, it was rare for anyone in the study to say that they had one-on-one conversations with him as Smith did. In fact, Smith was one of only three people who said they had any direct contact with Brashear. So, while Smith was not a principal leader, he was a high-status leader. That he regarded Brashear as iconic and easily submitted to his authority further affirms Brashear's status as a principal leader.

Another black religious leader, Michael Wood, supported Smith's view of Brashear. He said

> Wyoming Brashear, . . . you're going to respect that name. . . . You know . . . when he speaks, it doesn't really have anything to do with denomination or that kind of—you're just going to respect who [he] is. . . . He's like when Fred Shuttlesworth was alive. . . . When Fred Shuttlesworth spoke, I mean, it didn't matter if you were Pentecostal or whatever you were, you just listened because he spoke. [*Laughs*] You know what I mean?

Similar to Smith, Wood elevated Brashear to a leader among leaders. According to him, Brashear's influence was broad, reaching across denominational lines. He also assigned Brashear iconic status, equating him to Rev. Fred Shuttlesworth, a central figure in the civil rights movement. Wood corroborated Smith's claim that other black religious leaders listened to what Brashear said, explaining, with a chuckle, that "when [Brashear] speaks, . . . you just listened."

Whereas Wood equated Brashear's influence to that of Fred Shuttlesworth, Reed Irvine explicitly noted Brashear's participation in the civil rights movement and ties to two powerful figures in the US sociopolitical landscape, Dr. Martin Luther King Jr. and President Bill Clinton. When asked who the influential black religious leaders were, Irvine responded,

> Oh, well, to this day, it's still Wyoming Brashear. . . . He had been part of the civil rights movement with Dr. King and knew him personally. And, um, Bill Clinton, and you know those types of persons have been to his church, and . . . his influence, you know, spans several cities and several decades. . . . His name . . . carries weight in the black religious and political community.

Not only was Brashear perceived as being connected to important, powerful figures, but it is reasonable to posit, if we take Irvine's information as credible, that powerful politicians perceived Brashear as an important, powerful figure. Moreover, Brashear's influence was understood by Irvine to be enduring, spanning time, and far reaching, spanning geographic space. While it is difficult to imagine what would constitute greater influence than simply being able to say the word and know that others will do as you request, the extent of Brashear's influence did not stop there, at least according to Irvine. He added that black religious leaders not only responded to what Brashear said but, apparently, responded to his name as well. Brashear's name "carries weight," as he put it. This suggests that others could say that Wyoming Brashear supported an issue, and that alone was sufficient for people to support it.

Not surprisingly, with descriptions like these, it became clear that Wyoming Brashear was an important person in the black religious leader network. I, the lead author, pursued an interview with him. He agreed. After hearing about the breadth of Brashear's influence, I expected that he would exude self-importance. However, this was not the case. On the contrary, I found Brashear to be quite gracious and humble. He was eloquent and could tell an engaging story. His mannerisms were smooth and his laugh easy. In a word, he struck me as secure.

This security extended to his status as a principal leader. Brashear knew perfectly well that he was highly influential among black religious leaders and beyond. He recounted a story in the interview about when the OFA campaign asked him to be one of its informal advisers and facilitate voter mobilization in the state. OFA repeatedly attempted to get black religious leaders to help mobilize the vote but to no avail. The campaign learned that it needed help accessing the black religious leader community and reached out to Brashear. Brashear, who at this time held no formal clergy position, agreed to provide it. He explained why he was asked and what he did to help:

> For one, I happen to know a lot of people, a lot of pastors, . . . across the nation. Some of the young people involved . . . in the campaign didn't know any[one]. . . . And I could say to them, "When you go to Columbus, Ohio, be sure to check in with ABCD. . . . Tell them what you need. . . . And if you want to, you can tell them I sent you. [*Laughs*] Uh, and, I'm sure you will get support."

Brashear's claim that he was well connected with the local and national black religious leader networks as well as other networks across the country was confirmed by a simple Google search. He was featured on many website postings affiliated with organizations or outlets from around the country. Google showed over thirteen thousand sites that came up after searching his name. Additionally, just as Irvine suggested, Brashear's name "carried weight." Brashear's story of the way he helped OFA operatives illustrates how. It was surprisingly simple. He told OFA workers to contact a select few local pastors, explain to them what they needed, and, while doing so, be sure to let them know that Wyoming Brashear sent them. Brashear was sure the pastors would do as the OFA workers requested.

Brashear also warned OFA workers what would happen if they did not follow his direction:

> If you go to such-and-such a town, . . . you've got to check in with ABC if you want to get off the ground. . . . Now, after you get your organization going, you can, you know, do a lot of things, but you're going to get blocked if [*laughs*] you don't at least acknowledge their being, . . . uh, because they do know a lot of folks. . . . And if they are cold, folks will sit down, but if they are enthusiastic, folks will participate.

Here, Brashear outlined for OFA the structure of the black religious leader network. Not only were there principal leaders in the black religious leader community, of which he was one. Principal leaders sat atop an informal, hierarchical structure. Outsiders would be unaware of this structure and how it worked. However, for those who wanted to build relationships with black religious leaders, it was critically important that they understood the structure of the network, specifically how they ought to approach it. Brashear made it clear that if the right people were not "enthusiastic" about a matter, the rest of the community would not be either. He stressed that "you've *got* to check in with ABC"; otherwise "you're going to get blocked" (emphasis added). This was a clear, unequivocal statement. Either you go through the proper channels or expect to pay a hefty price: total or near total exclusion from the black religious leader community.

Mark Thompson also emerged as a principal leader of the black religious leaders in Ohio. I gathered from the way other leaders interacted with him at the denominational get-out-the-vote session that he was someone of importance and pursued an interview with him. Yet, despite his observable influence over other leaders, it was learned from the interview with Thompson that he had to exert considerably more energy than Brashear to assert authority over other religious leaders. We attribute this to the strength of his civil rights movement credentials. Unlike Brashear, Thompson did not actually participate in the civil rights movement. He was, however, mentored by civil rights movement activists and leaders.

Thompson compensated for deficiencies in his civil rights movement credentials with other skills and resources. He was a broker (Burt 2004), which meant that he was a gatekeeper to resources critical for mobilization and the conduit through which these resources flowed. Brokers also possess a diverse portfolio of cultural capital as a result of exposure to varying social networks (Diani 2003; Stovel and Shaw 2012; Padgett and Ansell 1993). As a result of having been actively engaged in mobilization for several decades, Thompson accumulated extensive mobilization experience and knowledge. He also built a broad network that cut across a variety of religious and civic organizations facilitating what Michael Lindsay (2008) calls "convening power," which allowed him to bring people from across sectors and communities together. And like movement entrepreneurs (Jenkins 1983; McCarthy and Zald 1977, 2002), he had the ability to frame a grievance and mobilize people around a cause, as was seen in chapter 1.

Thompson first got engaged in "the movement," as he put it, while an undergraduate student at an HBCU in the South. It was there that he was mentored by and worked for Henry Lipkins, a civil rights movement icon. He continued organizing in graduate school, during which time he got the opportunity to be mentored by and work with yet another civil rights movement icon, Pastor Ronald Temple, because, Thompson explained, Temple "took a liking to me, and so I ended up working for him." When Thompson returned to Ohio after college, he said, "I was young, had heart, had courage, and . . . had a sense of the issues. You know . . . and just came back running, and I've been sort of running ever since." Thompson characterized this activist approach as being "like a . . . lawyer riding around town, just, you know, trying to find an accident."

Along his journey, Thompson worked with an array of organizations. He pastored or worked with religious organizations affiliated with historically black denominations, mainline Protestantism, and conservative Protestantism. Encouraged by one of his mentors, he started a local chapter of a national civic organization and had been actively involved with another. He held a formal leadership position in the local chapter of an FBCO and was an activist leader with another. He was also one of a small number of religious leaders who formed a local interdenominational ministerial alliance of black pastors.

Thompson's extensive experience, breadth of connections, and organizational skills drew the attention of a national civic organization, Citizens for Civic Power (CCP). CCP invited him to help it with voter mobilization. He explained that "the [black pastors organizational arm] of CCP . . . chose [multiple] cities across the country to work through the black church to empower the vote": "I think . . . I probably was their number one [organizer]. . . . I was invited [by CCP] to [do] a debriefing on [our] voter project." A decade or so later, he became a board member and trainer with the black pastors group of CCP, participating in the strategy and direction of this arm of the organization, which had about five hundred black pastors nationwide, many of whom were located in politically important cities and states across the country.

Thompson had had legendary mentors as well as considerable experience as a leader and activist. He also developed an extensive, diverse social network. But was he a principal leader? When asked who were the most influential and active persons among black religious leaders, one pastor put it this way: "Pastor Thompson [wears] those different hats. He . . . gives very strong leadership to the sociopolitical issues that are before us." Another simply said that he is "one of the main network persons." However, the people Thompson hand selected to be his fellow "chief organizers," as he referred to them, were best suited to explain his leadership role among black religious leaders. One of them, Leroy McCutcheon, explained how Thompson recruited them to mobilize:

> One day Pastor Thompson called me and said that someone was coming into town, that he would like for me to meet here. His name is Tate Olson [a staff person with the national headquarters of CCP]. From that meeting with him there, Olson invited us to a meeting that they were having in Washington, during the Congressional Black Caucus meetings, . . . myself, Pastor Thompson, and two other pastors, Pastor Robert Burns and Pastor Anthony Jenkins. We come back, and we've been running ever since. . . . It's just been a—wow—it's been a whirlwind.

Here, Thompson was able to bring leaders of disparate social networks together. He then leveraged these links to mobilize black religious leaders to get engaged in mobilizing the vote. McCutcheon also made it clear why Thompson was their leader: "He is very seasoned in [mobilization]. I mean, he worked with Henry Lipkins and Ronald Temple. So this is—this is what he does. So, you know, we leaned heavily on his expertise—to help us, guide us, through the [voter-mobilization] project." We see from McCutcheon's description that Thompson was a principal leader for two reasons. One, he had a lot of experience with and knowledge about mobilizing. Two, he worked with two civil rights movement leader icons. Thus, black religious leaders relied on Thompson "heavily" for direction and guidance.

Brashear's and Thompson's stories provide insight into how they came to be principal leaders. Their stories also provide a window into the anatomy of the black religious leader structure, which we discuss next.

Anatomy of the Leader Structure

Social network characteristics like size, strength of connections, and elite influence matter for mobilization (Siegel 2009). The network of black religious leaders is no different. In our study, black religious leaders had at least three tiers: principal leaders, high-status leaders, and other leaders. The glue that held the network together was the value placed on what they simply called "relationships." It was high-status leaders who were particularly keen to emphasize the importance of relationship for black religious leaders. This is perhaps because without civil rights movement credentials, the main resource they had to sustain their high status was relationships. Jackson Smith simply stated, "It's all relationship. It's all relationship. We're all busy. . . . We will do things based on relationship, even if we don't have time." Another high-status black religious leader, Ruben Jones, similarly described this process, saying to the interviewer, with a slightly impatient tone, "I told you it was a network. You know, I mean all of us were networking kings. . . . So it was just— when you are into something and you are baptized in it, it becomes the norm." Rick Richardson tangentially interjected a story about his connections with high-status black civic and business leaders, saying, "It's relational, because what are we? We're relationship driven." Smith's, Jones's, and Richardson's uncomplicated, matter-of-fact descriptions of the process of mobilization reveal that there was an understanding within the network that "relationships" and "networking" were critical. This was normative, as Jones explicitly stated, just how things got done.

It was not simply relationships that mattered. It was the trust and density of the network—in others words, social capital—that was critical. As Rick Richardson put it, it got you "access" when aiming to achieve civic goals. He went on to explain, "Access is sometimes more important than even the authority. If that person doesn't have the authority, if they can make a phone call and say you're going to get a call, . . . that becomes important." And how does someone get "access"? Richardson explained, "Access comes by relationship. . . . If you have favor with a person in the church, they can, if you will, broker that favor to get you access to a person."

As with most critical resources, social capital is limited. Jackson Smith suggested that high-status leaders were aware of this reality. Addressing a question about how they would decide to pursue an issue, Smith explained that they first deliberated over an issue, posing several questions to themselves, like "What should we do? . . . Is this an issue for us to deal with? . . . Is this something we need to? Is this worthy of? Is it something we have to address? . . . Because," Smith added, "you don't have to address every issue." Smith drew on a very useful analogy to illustrate this point:

> I think that . . . sometimes we don't understand. . . . Young pastors [do] not understand . . . a basic principle. . . . When you go to a church, . . . that young pastor has what he calls "change" in his or her pocket. . . . You . . . go with a pocket full of change, and . . . so you do something and it doesn't work out. . . . But it's all right. None of them vote you out because you've got some change in your pockets still. So you can pay that. [You] say, "Okay . . . it was a mistake. That . . . cost me a little bit." And then you go down the road and do a little misstep, and you mess up again. They're not going to vote you out because you've still got change in your pocket. Now, here's what most—a lot of these preachers don't realize, if you're always putting change out of your pocket and never putting any in, one day you're going to run out. [*Laughs*] . . . You know, you're going to deplete it. And the same thing is true with the influence. . . . You know, if . . . you're always out there and everything's an issue, you . . . deplete your resources. You use up all the change in your pocket. . . . So you have to be judicious . . . in the use of your influential power.

There are several takeaways from Smith's description. What is quite clear is that black religious leaders were keenly aware of the value of social capital and that it was not a limitless resource. It was important to consider how to use their social capital—or "influential power"—if they wanted to get a return on the issues in which they chose to invest. At worst, they did not want to deplete their social capital. It was important to protect. Additionally, the decisions about what issues to address were made collectively. Decisions were not made unilaterally, unless, of course, you were a principal leader, as we have discussed. Smith implied that established black religious leaders understood this economy. However, young pastors may not. His metaphor suggests that he had witnessed young pastors come to their churches eager and ready to make change, aiming to tackle issue after issue without sufficient support from their congregations. If a pastor consistently moved forward without the support of their community, they would eventually lose the trust of their congregants and perhaps their job. Smith's analogy also suggests that seasoned pastors knew that they, not just young pastors, were also accountable to their congregations. He did not say this explicitly, but it stands to reason that they too had to be prudent about what causes in which to involve their congregants. The power of the congregants to vote pastors out would loom and perhaps keep all pastors in check, not just young ones.

As already seen in pastors' descriptions of Thompson and Brashear, the hierarchical nature of their network was (generally) accepted and respected. The hierarchy cut across denominational and other organizational lines, giving principal leaders a breadth of influence. Smith and Brashear were not a part of the same denomination. Neither were Thompson and McCutcheon. Neither were Brashear and Thompson for that matter. But how did the hierarchy work if it was not dependent on formal bureaucratic structures?

Brashear began to provide some insight into this question. He did not contact all the pastors he knew in the network when he wanted to mobilize black religious leaders. He provided direction to only a select few who were high-status leaders. Recall him telling OFA workers, "When you go to [city], be sure to *check in with ABCD*" (emphasis added). He told them to lend his direction to only a small number of people who were understood to be most influential in their local area.

One of these people was Jackson Smith, who outlined how the hierarchy worked from his position in the network. He explained that he may receive a call from Brashear (or someone representing Brashear) who will say something like, "Hey, listen. We're going to be on the line [a conference call]. . . . It's going to be about six of us." Smith interjected his hypothetical conversation here, saying, "And see, you—you kind of know, based on how many are on the call, how really important it is. Because if it's three, four, five, six, then you know, 'Hey, these are hand-picked people.'" He continued, "Then—then they step in and say, 'Okay, now we've got to get more people on.' And then, in that group, there may be twenty-five people. Then, the next one, and you can have fifty or sixty people on a conference call. But the first call is calling to a smaller group.

And then we say, 'Okay, who else needs to be on the call next?' And go from there." The interviewer asked Smith if this was common, to which he simply responded, "Sure." He went on to explain that when he got these sorts of calls, the person on the line would start off the conversation saying, "Hey, there's an issue. We need to deal with this."

Rick Richardson was another high-status leader. He shared how he experienced the informal hierarchy from his location in the network. In his description of the voter-mobilization efforts, he explained, "What happened with clergy [in the get-out-the-vote efforts], there were a lot of conference calls with national folk and clergy . . . to make sure that we understood the importance of this election, getting folks out, our role in that, making sure the issues were clear. . . . And like almost every Monday for six weeks there were conference calls." A little later in the conversation he went on to say, "Everybody was kind of charged with following up with some of the guys who may not have made that list [people on the conference call] but guys in the community who you knew had influence." The interviewer asked, "How many people were on the conference call?" He responded, "Oh, I don't know, probably fifty or sixty."

Taken together, Brashear's, Smith's, and Richardson's accounts of how black religious leaders were mobilized and their roles in the process provide an outline of the network's hierarchical structure. It began with a principal leader, who called a small number of high-status black religious leaders who were "handpicked" and "influential." Then, after explaining to them the "issue" at hand, the principal leader and this first small group of select pastors decided on the next set of people to be brought in on the conversation. This process went through additional iterations, ultimately moving from a very small group of three to six people to a conference call as large as "fifty or sixty" people. These fifty or sixty leaders were then charged with sharing the information provided during the large group conference call with, as Richardson explained, "some of the guys who may not have made that list but guys in the community who [they] knew had influence." Finally, there were those who had little to no influence in the leader network. The data suggest that these black religious leaders were mobilized at conferences and meetings.

A hierarchical network structure was also used by Mark Thompson to mobilize black religious leaders. Yet it functioned differently for Thompson. Recall that McCutcheon explained that Thompson asked him and two other pastors to be his chief organizers in the effort to mobilize the black vote. There are two key points we want to highlight. The first is that Thompson, like Brashear, picked a select group of high-status pastors to assist him in the mobilization effort, and they responded to his call. The selection of these "chief organizers" was surely strategic, based on their potential influence, just as Brashear's selection was. McCutcheon held a high-status position in his denomination. He was also already moving among Democratic political circles. He explained in his interview that he was regularly invited to exclusive political events and dinners. So he had already begun to develop ties to important networks and gained some visibility outside the black religious leader network. Burns, one of the other two chief organizers (who also participated in this study), was the president of a local interdenominational ministerial alliance. And Jenkins served on local civic and political boards and panels. Thompson was able to get these pastors to invest considerable energy and time in mobilization efforts, pastors who were, in their own right, already high status, further revealing Thompson's status as a principal leader.

Do Principal Leaders Matter?

To understand the norms and values of a community, it is helpful to draw on the perspectives of those who are part of that community as well as those outside it who desire to build relationships with that community. So far, the experiences and perspectives of the black religious leaders in this study reveal that they look to certain peers for direction. Interviews with the civic leaders who worked with or wanted to work with them provide further insight into the role of the principal leader and how that role helps us understand the black religious leader network. The civic leaders' experiences suggest that their capacity to work with the black religious leader network depended on their knowledge about the unspoken informal hierarchical structure that organized it.

Take, for example, the testimony of Samuel Lyons, who was the president of a local chapter of a civic organization. He described having a close relationship with a local black denominational alliance in his city. Particularly interesting is his account of how he navigated relationships with black clergy in this organization:

The president of [a local black denominational alliance], as I stated, is
Rev. Leonard Wilson, and one of the things that we allow—not just allow but expect—is that he's the leader of that organization. We don't set
their agenda. We provide information to them about issues, and then
he communicates that information to the clergy that follow him in the
denominational alliance. So [we have] some relationships—like Pastor
Arnold here locally, who we're very close with. A gentleman by the name
of Rev. Ricketts does a phenomenal job. They're all members of the alliance. But, again, those relationships *always* go through their president,
period! (emphasis added)

Lyons outlined how he experienced and understood the way that the
black religious leader community functioned. He recognized that the
local alliance established its agenda and made it clear that it did not come
from outsiders. He repeatedly noted that his organization respected the
position of Wilson, the alliance's president. It was critical, in his view,
that an outsider not be perceived as trying to undermine Wilson. What
is particularly striking about Lyons's description is that even though
he had "close" relationships with other members of the alliance, he
understood that those relationships "always go through their president,
period!" Lyons did not see himself as having a series of independent
relationships with multiple black religious leaders. Instead, he had a set
of relationships that was channeled through one person, a high-status
black religious leader.

This story of a relationship between a leader of a civic organization
and that of a local black denominational alliance begins to illustrate how
the black religious leader community was structured. It was important
that civic leaders who wanted to partner with black religious leaders in
the state had an understanding of how the community operated. Their
ability to successfully access the resources embedded in the community
depended on it. This becomes all the more clear when we contrast Lyons's experience to that of Jerome Nichols, an African American leader
of an FBCO.

Nichols also aimed to mobilize black churches in the same city as
Lyons. Typically, organizers in the FBCO tradition directly and inde-
pendently engage head clergy of churches. Pastors, lay leaders, and paid
organizing staff together decide on agendas (Warren 2001; Wood 2002).

This approach, though, was not amenable to the structure of the black religious leader community, as Nichols learned. He explained, "So, in [our city], we have some competition in this work, if you will. The national civic organization [headed by Lyons] does a lot of voter registration work, and . . . they are connected with a lot of African American churches. So there are a lot of churches that work with them instead of with us." This statement corroborates Lyons's account of his experience, that he was able to work with black religious leaders in the city. Nichols's observation also suggests that he perceived his organization to be in competition with other civic organizations for church resources. Moreover, he believed that black religious leaders were choosing between his and other organizations. It did not dawn on him that perhaps his approach to the community of black religious leaders was the problem.

Nichols noticed that OFA also had more success in mobilizing black pastors than his organization did. He recalled,

> It's an interesting dynamic that there were a lot more black pastors who got involved in the get-out-the-vote work when OFA came through. They had an ability to activate people that we approached and would not work with us. So that is something that has been really a challenge to me to think about. . . . What is it that they're able to do to connect with black churches in a way that we weren't able to?

Nichols's organization attempted to "activate" black religious leaders to mobilize voters during the 2012 election. While the organization had some success, it was minimal. His organization approached black religious leaders about collaborating in voter-mobilization efforts, but they did not accept the offer. These same leaders did, however, work with OFA. As Nichols saw it, "[OFA] had an ability to activate people that we approached and would not work with us." This was quite perplexing to him. He recognized that he was missing *something* and rhetorically asked, "What is it that they're able to do to connect with black churches in a way that we weren't able to?" Nichols presumed that it had to do with what OFA was "able to do," its "ability," that made it more successful. This was not the case, as we learned from Wyoming Brashear. Nichols and his organization were outsiders who did not understand the culture and structure of the black religious leader community. They were not missing some skill or knowledge but relationships with the right people. Consequently, they were denied access to the black religious leader network's mobilizing capacity.

The Limits of the Civil Rights Movement Credential

The civil rights movement credential mattered to the black religious leaders in our study. The value placed on the civil rights movement implies that black religious leaders in the study valued civic and political rights. They also identified with and valued the legacy of the accomplishments of the black religious leaders involved in the movement. Possessing the civil rights movement credential made people eligible to be principal leaders in the black religious leader network. The hierarchical, socially dense structure of the network made it possible for them to then have considerable and broad influence over the black religious leader network and sustain the power their status afforded them once gained.

We see this with Brashear and Thompson. They were empowered because of their connection to the civil rights movement in some tangible way, either as a result of direct engagement in the movement or because of a close relationship with those who were. So, when they ask their peers to engage in voter mobilization, they do. However, voter mobilization is consistent with a goal and accomplishment of the civil rights movement: blacks' expanded access to the vote. Brashear's and Thompson's peers were perhaps inclined to follow their direction when it came to voter mobilization because this reinforced the legacy of the civil rights movement and their understanding of what it means to be a quintessential black religious leader, a priest that is also a prophet who fights for the rights of blacks and against any threats to them.

Could Brashear or Thompson mobilize their peers for an effort that was not consistent with the goals and aims of the civil rights movement? We are unable to directly address this question. We can reasonably speculate that their power was constrained. As noted, there was no evidence of black religious leaders involved in broad mobilization, that is, mobilization that was sustained over an extended period time (over a year) and across the state, for any issue within the past five years of the study, except voter mobilization. They commonly reported working with a small number of their peers on a specific local issue, like attracting retail to their neighborhoods, supporting local schools, or pressuring local governments to hire minority contractors. This is surprising, particularly given the national context at the time of the interviews. As already noted, a majority of the interviews for this study was conducted less than a year after the death of Trayvon Martin. Considerable national fervor around the systemic pattern of unjust deaths of unarmed black people across the country had already emerged by this time. Yet this issue barely registered in the interviews as an important issue for which black religious leaders should mobilize. And neither Brashear nor Thompson even broached using their power to harness what Morris (1984, 11) calls the "collective power of churches" to address this or any systemic form of racism or racial discrimination. We turn to unpacking this inattention further in chapter 4.

Another challenge with valuing civil rights movement credentials is that the generation of civil rights movement pastors will soon no longer be with us. Even those who are younger than they are whom they mentored in the movement are getting older. What will this do to the mobilizing capacity of the black religious leader network? If black religious leaders do not change how they understand themselves as both priests to their congregants and also prophets to the world, will they lose their power as a prophetic voice and an agent for social change in the twenty-first century? Will they lose their ability to engage in broad mobilization efforts, even voter mobilization, as no one will have the qualifications to initiate and lead such an effort? We cannot know the future, but these are critical questions that black religious leaders must grapple with and address—and quickly—if they want to maintain any social or civic influence not only in the African American community but in society at large.

4

The Black Protestant Ethic

So far, we have focused on black religious leaders' voter-mobilization efforts as a lens through which to understand why they engage in broad mobilization efforts and how they go about doing it. We were also interested in their perspectives on other social issues, namely, those that affect blacks in the United States. We asked black religious leaders if they thought there were social problems that are unique to blacks and how these problems could be addressed. Nearly all said they believed blacks' socioeconomic disadvantage had to do with structural factors, often citing institutional racism and racial discrimination. This is consistent with other work (e.g., Lincoln and Mamiya 1990; Pinn 2002; McDaniel 2003, 2008). However, we found that a slight majority drew on internal explanations as well, locating both the problem of black disadvantage and its solution in the agency of black individuals or blacks more broadly. In other words, blacks' disadvantage lies with blacks themselves or the culture of blacks generally. These internally focused explanations almost always coexisted with structural ones. However, when the black religious leaders were given the opportunity to offer more concrete reasons and solutions for black-white inequities, a significant proportion turned to internal ones.

Notably, it was black religious leaders who were a part of largely white denominations who were more inclined to draw on internal explanations for racial inequality. This is not particularly surprising. Whites are generally more likely than blacks to draw on internal explanations for racial inequality (Emerson and Smith 2000; Shelton and Emerson 2012). It is reasonable to expect black religious leaders who are embedded in predominantly white religious communities to be influenced by the values, beliefs, and attitudes prevalent in those circles. Nevertheless, even though black churches affiliated with black denominations are found to be the most engaged in resistance activism (Brown 2006; Cavendish 2002; Chaves and Higgins 1992; Beyerlein and Chaves 2003), in this study, a substantial proportion of black religious leaders across religious affiliations, including many who were affiliated with black denominations, believed that the cause and solution to black subordination is, in part, because of blacks, as individuals or a group.

This finding is perhaps surprising to some readers. Black religious leaders, especially those affiliated with the black church, maintain a reputation for having a high racial consciousness and commitment to social justice (McDaniel 2003, 2008; Shelton and Emerson 2012; Barnes and Nwosu 2014). However, their views on social inequities, especially those affecting African Americans, are not so simple. Our findings suggest that today's dominant racial narrative has also influenced the social perspectives of contemporary black religious leaders too, so that even a good proportion of them do not see social structure as being the central reason for the social inequities that disproportionately disadvantage blacks in the United States. To these black religious leaders, African Americans have bootstraps. They just need to find them.

On African American Inequities

We are not going to focus on what black religious leaders we spoke with had to say about systemic or institutional explanations here. Considerable work has examined this issue. We focus rather on their internal explanations for black-white social inequity. The internal explanations that black religious leaders provided can be grouped into two broad categories: personal irresponsibility and family dysfunctions. Personal irresponsibility includes behaviors or attitudes that do not recognize one's own or one's group's agency or culpability in their suffering. Whether it is the individual or the culture of African Americans, personal irresponsibility explanations say that blacks experience disadvantages because they or their group are in some way irresponsible. It is ultimately incumbent on blacks, in no small part, to rectify the social problems they experience. Generally, two explanations for family dysfunction were given. One was poor socialization of youth. Parents do not properly socialize their children, teaching them what is needed to succeed in life. The second explanation had to do with deviation from the patriarchal, traditional family structure. Black religious leaders who drew on this explanation of family dysfunction were especially concerned about black males. We turn to personal irresponsibility first.

Personal Irresponsibility

Mike Williams, who headed a church affiliated with a black denomination, emphasized the importance of personal responsibility. He made several points in his response to the question of solutions for black disadvantage, but they all return to personal responsibility in one manner or another. He said, "So, from a standpoint of a leader, I think that we need to be honest with our people. . . . Teaching individual responsibility—nobody wants to hear [what I have to say] on individual responsibility. . . . We're missing the boat as black leaders by not teaching or emphasizing [this]." Williams believed it was the job of pastors to teach their congregants the importance of individual responsibility. Pastors and congregants, he implied, did not want to discuss the possibility that African Americans' social and economic hardship could be simply due to irresponsibility. The pastors, in particular, were "missing the boat" on this matter, according to him, misunderstanding the real issue. As he noted, nobody wanted to hear what he had to say about this, suggesting that he had attempted to introduce the importance of teaching individual responsibility in contexts with other African American pastors and was rebuffed. While this claim cannot be corroborated by other data in the study, this pastor seemed to believe that there was a culture among black religious leaders in which irresponsibility as an explanation for social inequality was taboo.

Williams then moved from talking about the need for religious leaders to teach their congregants about individual responsibility to talking about the need for people to assume responsibility for personal matters. He drew on two examples in which someone requested, perhaps of him or his church, financial assistance with paying bills or buying food. He continued,

> At the end of the day, you're the one who's going to be hungry, not me. You're the one with your lights cut off, not me. So, if I can't teach you individual responsibility, saying, "Listen, I know the house is chilly, but maybe you ought to put on some more clothes and turn that thermostat

down, because at the end of the month, [the gas company] is going to come looking for their money. I mean, you've got to take responsibility. I can't do this for you."

In his view, people could not pay their bills or buy food because they had misplaced priorities. They used their money to purchase nonessentials, like clothes or comfort in the form of an unnecessarily warm home. It was not because they were too poor to cover the costs of their expenses. It was that they chose to spend their money on what they wanted and then asked others to compensate for where they came up short in paying their expenses.

Lou Davis, who headed a large congregation affiliated with a black denomination, focused on the unequal treatment black men experience at the hands of police officers. He did not place the blame of this ill treatment on a racially unjust, abusive criminal justice system. He rather proposed that the solution to addressing police harassment lay with the black men getting harassed. He explained,

I believe that brothers set themselves up for harassment. If you are on the corner, . . . you're a dope boy—what they call it—and that's what you do all day. Then you put yourself to be a target of harassment by police officers or anybody, because you're standing there looking like there's nothing—[like] you don't have anything to do. So my belief, if we can work to get the guys off the street and get them employment, then they'll be less guys on the street, less harassment. . . . I've seen guys in my church who go from not having a job to having a job. And there is a twinkle in an African American man's eyes when he is working . . . and to do it legally.

Black men who stood on the corner, who were drug dealers or at least appeared to be, made themselves a "target" by "standing there looking like there's nothing . . . to do." The primary problem, then, was being too visible and appearing indolent to police. Davis recognized that "legal" employment would decrease the odds of a person spending consider-able time "on the corner." He also saw employment as a way to increase the confidence of a person, when he said working gives "a twinkle in an African American man's eyes." But he did not suggest what changes needed to occur in the workforce to eliminate racial discrimination and open up employment opportunities for African Americans, men in particular. He turned the responsibility inward, stating, "if we can work to get the guys off the street and get them employment, then they'll be less guys on the street, less harassment." The impetus for change, at least in part, starts with the "we." We took this to be either blacks broadly or black pastors more narrowly. Either way, the solution to minimizing police harassment was internal. Blacks needed to make themselves less of a target by avoiding hanging out on corners appearing to have nothing to do. His group, the "we," had to engage in strategies to help these men get jobs.

Explanations related to responsibility, at both the individual and group level, were given also by Timothy Mullins, a pastor who too headed a congregation affiliated with a black denomination:

> In the black church . . . we have to promote black business. . . . You know, if [you] have young men who are starting up moving companies or whatever, we have to promote that. We have to tell our people, you know, "Listen, this is out there," you know. You know, "Try to give them a shot." But then I think we have to hold . . . their feet to the fire too. We have to tell them, "Listen, now. I'm going to promote you. You ought to do a good job. You know what I mean? If your hours of the business are from 9:00 until 5:00, then, you know, I can't refer people to you and you're not getting into the office until 11:00." You understand what I mean? If there's going to be colored folk mess, then, [*laughs*] you know, I can't promote it, if you're not going to be professional.

There are several layers of responsibility here. It was the responsibility of the black church to promote its own by supporting black-owned businesses. It was his responsibility as a pastor in the black church to encourage others in his congregation to support these businesses. And individuals starting businesses must be responsible entrepreneurs. However, the black church should hold them accountable for doing a "good job" by "holding their feet to the fire." What is a bad job? One example is holding undependable business hours, saying you are open from "9:00 until 5:00 and . . . not getting into the office until 11:00." This example of business culture was not only unprofessional for this pastor but endemic to black culture, what he called "colored folk mess." The consequence of engaging in "colored folk mess" is that a pastor should not promote the person's business in the black church. Given that a function of religious organizations is building advantageous social ties and that black pastors are afforded considerable esteem in black churches, such a consequence could diminish the likelihood of a successful business.

George Bass, who headed a smaller church affiliated with a predominantly white denomination explained that race mattered for African Americans a century ago but, today, racial inequality is more of an "economic problem," even though it might appear to be racial. He said, "I think although we may have a racial problem, as DuBois said of the twentieth century, that *seems* true of the twenty-first century. I think it really is grounded in an economic problem. It just affects us disproportionately because of the systemic structures and our systemic challenges that we face." He went on to say, "We [blacks] don't hold any wealth. We make income. We consume everything; we don't produce anything."

Bass attributed disproportionate socioeconomic disadvantage experienced by blacks to economics, not race. The inward focus of his explanation was more subtle than the others presented thus far. It actually has to do with the extremeness of his claims, particularly in the second part of his explanation, where he said, "We [blacks] consume everything. We don't produce anything." Of course, this was an exaggeration. Yet at its core remains an insistence that blacks as a group use their agency to consume rather than to contribute to the growth of the economy. Underlying this perception is a judgment that blacks are on the whole monetarily irresponsible, and this irresponsibility exacerbates the economic disadvantages that they already disproportionately experience. Moreover, there is an unspoken comparison to other racial groups that he assumes are much less consumer oriented and more productive than blacks are.

The next pastor, Justin Green, who was particularly active in get-out-the-vote efforts in his city and who was considered a high-status pastor among his peers, used internal explanations for inequities that blacks experience. Discussing voter-suppression tactics, he said,

> I said the night after the Sunday after the election, "We're going to continue voter education." I said, "Number one, y'all moving too damn much." Black folks' problem is that they move too much. "You move too

much, and then you ought to have sense enough to know if you moved, where you used to live, and go back down there and vote and don't be coming up with all these provisional stuff and this." Please. And so we're working on stuff like that, just the basics. Just the—if we would just do the basic stuff.

Green believed that blacks were, in part, easily susceptible to voter-suppression tactics because of cultural patterns and characteristics, namely, high levels of residential mobility and limited knowledge about how the voting process works. He went on to say, "You know, you got a generation of people who were sired by a generation of people who don't know." We see that he further attributed blacks' susceptibility to poor socialization and ignorance, especially among younger blacks. This perspective on the cultural and structural characteristics of recent generations of blacks suggests he believed that the social problems experienced by contemporary blacks are in part self-inflicted. Relatively frequent residential mobility was framed as personal choice rather than being rooted in structural patterns.[1]

Family Structure Dysfunction

Family dysfunction was another reason given for black disadvantage. Take, for instance, Pastor Leroy Owens, whose church was affiliated with a black denomination. He believed poor education, which leads to workforce racial inequality, was a primary social problem among African Americans. This problem, though, was mainly the result of the "deterioration of the family." He explained,

> The education practice really has to start with the family at the very essence of a child that's in pre-K level—even before pre-K—understanding the importance of family and structures, you know, of building the kid up, giving them goals, aspirations, and dreams, exposing them, saying, "Hey," to the positive things. You know, "What do you want to be when you grow up?" And then helping them to formulate a practice to read, to write—uh, you know, starting at the very primary level. So all of that really centers around family. I believe starting at the youngest of age. To do that, it really will help. And then . . . as they grow, exposing them to dif-

ferent professions, versus, you know, "Just be athletes." You know, expose them to . . . doctors, surgeons.

For Owens, the family needs to give a child confidence ("build them up"), encourage them to think about their "goals, aspirations, and dreams" and what they "want to be when [they] grow up." The family should also teach children that there are more career options available to them than being an athlete, such as being a doctor or surgeon. Then, on top of this, the family can help teach children the fundamentals of education like reading and writing. The implication of his suggestion is that there are not enough African Americans who invest in their children in these ways.

Jeff Roberts headed a congregation affiliated with a predominantly white denomination. He discussed the role of the family for the educational and career outcomes of children as well, pointing to his own experience as an example:

My mom got to the eighth grade. My dad may have gotten to the sixth grade. And it wasn't an issue, whether I was going to go to college or not. I was going to go. I was the youngest of five children. Uh, neither of my four seniors—senior siblings—ever went to college. And I was blessed to be able to go, even though I took a roundabout way. It was primarily because my parents pushed me. And that's something that we, as African Americans, have to do.

Roberts went to college "primarily because [his] parents pushed [him]." He concluded from his experience that it was incumbent on more African American parents to have very high expectations of their children to go to college. Curiously, this pastor did not account for why his four older siblings did not go to college. Following the logic of his explanation, the reason would be that his parents did not push them to do so. Considering the broader context of his personal experience, it is perhaps that limited financial resources, low levels of education of his parents, and education structures that disadvantage working-class families and families of color produced a one-in-five "success" rate for his family. He was also the youngest. Being the last child may have meant the parents had more resources, in the form of knowledge or connections or money, to support a child in college by the time he was about to leave home. Yet this is not how he explained lower educational attainment among African Americans.

Greg Cook, who was affiliated with a black denomination, saw "economic issues" as problematic, although he was not convinced that this was a matter unique to blacks. He did see family stability as a particular challenge within the black community, saying,

> Well . . . I don't know whether uniqueness of it, but obviously you have economic issues. I think that, . . . you know, the family has definitely been an issue within our community, as far as keeping the family together, which then ties into economics as well. So I think that having stable families with, you know, steady income would totally change the face of black America, if we could have that be not the exception but the rule in our community. I think that's what has plagued us, you know, for decades is the disintegration of the family, . . . disintegration of economic opportunities. And, you know, it has a cascading effect.

As Cook saw it, "stable families . . . would totally change the face of black America." With stable families would come economic strength. Family structure is directly linked to the economic health of the family and thereby the broader community.

Responding to a follow-up question, Cook was initially unsure about solutions for addressing the disintegration of the family and, consequently, the economic issues experienced by blacks. Ultimately, he suggested multiple solutions. However, each of the solutions offered in the following excerpt are internal and demand changes by black people or churches:

> I wish I knew. . . . I think it comes into your expectation. You look at the media that our young people watch that really don't champion the family. You look at a lot of ways in which I think the churches even, not intentionally, . . . failed in some respects of really upholding the family, the traditional family in our community. And I think . . . there are things now that are . . . acceptable, that if we really stopped to think about it, that you know we really need to critique and think to change.

When he was asked, "What are some ways in which you think the church has not been helpful?" he answered,

> I think one thing is the schedule; staying in church all day. . . . If you look at a lot of our congregation's schedules, they're really geared toward elderly or single people. . . . [They're] really not conducive to working parents with children. . . . If you don't have certain resources, then this is not the place for you. And we say that without sayin' it, and I don't even think we realize it.

Poor or ineffective socialization was the primary obstacle to developing and sustaining stable families for this pastor. The media play a part. Young black people chose to watch television programs that did not "champion the family." By "family," he meant the traditional family. The churches were not helping either. The way in which church was done did not welcome, affirm, or facilitate family life. What could churches do? They could organize congregational life around families, that is, households composed of married working couples with children.

A particular concern of some pastors in this study was the experience of males in families, a concern we began to see in the explanations emphasizing the importance of personal and group-level responsibility. Kevin Miller, whose congregation was affiliated with a white-controlled denomination, began his response with broad solutions before he moved on to focus on what he perceived to be of particular concern for African Americans. Miller began his response by saying, "Well . . . I guess, you know, there's always the economic aspect and, I think, educational aspect. That may not be unique to African Americans, but certainly it's of great concern." Economic and educational challenges were important, but they were not necessarily unique to African Americans. He then homed in on the issue that he saw as a unique concern for African Americans, the high male incarceration rate:

> Almost 80 percent of African American prison populations—almost 80 percent of the males in those prisons—come from fatherless homes. And that . . . just devastates me. And to me, I think, that speaks loudly of, especially, African American churches that need to have much more involve-

ment in the lives of African American boys. And so we've developed and started a ministry that we call Redeem the Boys. And what we do is, once a month, the men in our church, we get together with the boys. . . . And we're trying to be there to help mentor the boys and to let them know that we want to be there, to be available for them when they find themselves just in need of somebody to talk to.

What is immediately evident is that this pastor's concerns about African Americans generally were male-centric. Miller was "devastated" by the incarceration rate of African American men. Rightly so. But he saw "fatherless homes" as the cause for the high rate of black male incarceration, not problems with the criminal justice system. The solution for the high black male incarceration rate was for African American churches to be more involved in the lives of boys. For his church's part, it hoped to help steer black boys off the path toward incarceration through a mentorship program that targeted boys in his church's community.

John Smith, affiliated with a black denomination, held a similar sentiment as Miller. He suggested that a primary reason for the social problems affecting African Americans was a lack of strong, engaged black men in African American communities and families. Although this pastor was not a high-status religious leader, as we define them, he enjoyed a modicum of prominence in his city, as indicated by his repeated presence in the media. So his voice carried greater weight than that of many other pastors interviewed. He said, "I think that we have to do a better job of raising up stronger men within our community, because I've seen no race of people—I think every race of people, they're as strong, really, as the men or as healthy as the men are. I think if we have stronger men, we'll have stronger families. If we have stronger families, we're going to have stronger communities." We see that men are the bedrock of society from Smith's perspective. Strong families and communities have strong men. The reason black families and communities suffer socially and economically is that they do not have enough of them. His solution was that black churches and black communities need to better socialize men to be masculine, as he put it, "rais[e] up stronger men."

* * *

The media often portray the black minister as an activist first, someone who rallies against injustice, and a pastor second. This image in many ways caricaturizes the black religious leader, reducing this role to a symbol of black America. In reality, black religious leaders (and their churches) have historically been a diverse group with a breadth of ideologies and theologies and varying perspectives about how to address social problems (DuBois [1903] 2008; Mays and Nicholson 1933; Frazier 1974; Lincoln and Mamiya 1990). Contemporary black religious leaders lean to the left on many sociopolitical issues, particularly on matters relevant to African Americans (McDaniel 2003). They tend to possess a structural lens through which they interpret social issues (Shelton and Emerson 2012). Yet contemporary black religious leaders are not by any means to the left in their views on all social issues (Edwards 2016). And broadly speaking, they have tended to be theologically conservative (Lincoln and Mamiya 1990). Our study suggests that a good proportion of them hold conservative views on social issues impacting blacks as well. Many black religious leaders adhere to what we call a *black Protestant ethic*: a moral framework that recognizes systemic black socioeconomic disadvantage but also describes disadvantage as a personal, cultural, or family problem and seeks solutions to this disadvantage in white, Western Protestantism that emphasizes black responsibility.

That a black religious leader might hold to a black Protestant ethic should come as no surprise and should even be expected. Scholars of the black church have long noted how accommodationist or otherworldly ideologies are threaded with theologies of freedom (DuBois 1903 [2003]; Frazier 1974; Lincoln and Mamiya 1990). Black religious leaders' Protestantism, whether that be associated with black denominations or otherwise, emerged out of white, Western Protestantism. White, Western Protestantism, especially the conservative tradition, is organized around an individualist worldview. When black religious leaders voice views such as "There is a twinkle in an African American man's eyes when he is working" or "I can't refer people to you and you're not getting into the office until 11:00" or "Maybe you ought to put on some more clothes and turn that thermostat down," they are affirming a Western Protestant belief system that places a high value on what is understood to be hard work, punctuality, and frugality, better known as the Protestant ethic. Similarly, when black religious leaders place considerable importance on the traditional family structure, they are affirming their affiliation with white American Protestantism more specifically. A high value and investment in a traditional family structure is a core emphasis within white American Protestantism, most avowedly conservative Protestantism (Woodberry and Smith 1998; Denton 2005). It is reasonable to expect any Protestant leader, regardless of their race, to assume these values at some level.

An emergent theme in this study is that black male religious leaders can have a strong black-male-centric orientation. There is a long history of this orientation in the black church (Morris 1984; Gilkes 1998; Higginbotham 1993). For people in this study, their black-male-centric orientation becomes evident in their concerns about black oppression and disadvantage. Their perspectives are either "neutral" or focus on black men. Black men, for example, need gainful employment. Black boys need to be mentored. Black men need to be taught how to assume the position of power in the black family and community. Black men need to be protected from the racist criminal justice system.

This tendency to highlight the struggles of black men treats black women as invisible bystanders to the racialized experiences of blacks. The oppression that black women experience in a white-supremacist system is seen as simply derivative of what black men experience because they are the main targets of the system. The implication is that solutions that minimize or eliminate the negative effects experienced by black men will also minimize or eliminate the negative effects experienced by black women. Ironically, the resources of black churches (e.g., material, cultural, or human) largely come from women, since they make up a significant majority of black churches. Yet a logic that implies that helping black men is helping black women suggests that any racial injustices experienced primarily by black women are not worth the resources embedded in black churches. Thus, social problems that disproportionately impact black women, like human trafficking, high eviction rates, or poverty, would receive relatively little, if any, attention.

It is surely worth targeting social problems that are particularly harmful to certain groups. However, a lens focused mainly on black men is not helpful for rectifying black oppression. We propose that the aim should first be dismantling structures of white supremacy. Systems of white supremacy, not the unique disadvantages of certain subgroups (e.g., black men or black women), are what keep whites as a group located in the dominant social position and people of color in subordinate ones.[2] This advantage looks like, for example, repeatedly receiving the benefit of the doubt when mistakes, missteps, or wrongs have been done; receiving support and mentorship; and having your culture—that is your language, values, norms, artifacts, and so on—validated as normal. So we should focus on these factors as much as or more than the many seismic shocks that ripple through society and disadvantage and oppress not only blacks but all people of color, regardless of gender or other systems of oppression. It is then that we can move toward producing a society where all people are affirmed as fully human.[3]

5

A Different Ballgame

In the civil rights movement, organizations were central. Key organizations included the Southern Christian Leadership Conference (SCLC), the Student Nonviolent Coordinating Committee (SNCC), the National Association for the Advancement of Colored People (NAACP), and the Committee on Racial Equality (CORE). The indigenous resources of the black community, and in particular the black church, were central to these organizations' mobilization capacity. Aldon Morris explains, "Churches provided the movement with an organized mass base; a leadership of clergymen largely economically independent of the larger white society and skilled in the art of managing people and resources; an institutionalized financial base through which protest was financed; and meeting places where the masses planned tactics and strategies and collectively committed themselves to the struggle" (1984, 4). One crucial factor contributing to the ability of black churches to mobilize resources for the civil rights movement is that they were financially independent from white-controlled institutions (McAdam 1982; Morris 1984; Andrews 2007). The independence of black-led organizations allowed black leaders to coordinate and pursue their own agenda without significant interference from whites.

Some of the civil-rights-movement-era black-centered (and usually black-led) civic organizations still exist today and maintain a presence in Ohio, such as the NAACP, the SCLC, and the Urban League. There is also the National Action Network (NAN), founded by Rev. Al Sharpton. Surprisingly, most of the religious leaders in our study were not deeply engaged with these black-centered civic organizations. We discuss some of the reasons for this in this chapter.

Another, more recent development is the rise and growth of a field known as faith-based community organizing. Faith-based community organizations (FBCOs) are multiracial coalitions of churches, as well as other faith communities, that use community-organizing methods to work on a variety of social justice issues. Several clergy we spoke with were involved with organizations of this type. However, many FBCOs are led by whites. And while FBCOs are funded in part by constituent churches, they are also reliant on predominantly white funding institutions such as the Catholic Campaign for Human Development (CCHD) and philanthropic foundations (Hall and Hall 1996; Oyakawa 2017). FBCOs pursue economic and racial justice goals that many black religious leaders support. However, tension and distrust can emerge, both between black religious leaders and FBCOs and within the black religious leader community, particularly when black churches contribute significant resources to campaigns that do not center the black community. The diversion of resources embedded within the black religious leader network to sources outside of it has important implications for if, when, how, and for what black religious leaders mobilize.

Black Civic Organizations

Given the important role that black-centered civic organizations played in the civil rights movement and the continuing importance of the civil rights movement in black religious leader networks, we expected to find high levels of involvement in these organizations among the black religious leaders in our study. However, this was not the case. Interviewees were clearly reluctant to speak ill of black-centered civic organizations and often hesitated when asked directly about them. Based on what they were willing to say, the general consensus seemed to be that they were effective "only in pockets," as one pastor put it. In Cleveland and Columbus, it emerged that the NAACP was not very influential at all at the time of the interviews. One pastor in Cleveland said, "Some would probably say that our [NAACP] chapter here is not relevant, sort of across the board." Another Cleveland pastor said, "I think their influence has waned over the years. And I think that with the new election of [a new president], they're gonna try to get reorganized and reenergized. I don't know if that's going to happen." While a couple of religious leaders spoke with tentative hope about revitalization efforts and new leadership, there was not a strong sense that the organization would be a central player in local politics at any point in the near future. In Cincinnati, the NAACP seemed to be more robust, in large part because of the leadership at the time of the interviews. However, the organization was struggling with internal conflict. One Cincinnati pastor reported, "It's pretty active but a lackluster group. It just doesn't have the same appeal they did when I was a young guy. . . . Too much infighting."

Religious leaders gave a variety of reasons for their lack of involvement in black-centered civic organizations. Many spoke about the time commitment involved in attending meetings as a major obstacle. Here is a representative quote from Joseph Butler: "We are aware of them, and they are aware of us, okay. Let me say it like that. . . . Most religious leaders have enough on our plates, so we're not maybe quite as involved or in depth with other organizations. We support them by membership, . . . as membership costs or dues or something of that nature. . . . You gotta choose what meetings you want to go to." If our interview data are any indication, it seems that in Ohio, black religious leaders were not choosing to go to meetings of black-centered civic organizations. Jason Armstrong spoke somewhat sheepishly about not attending SCLC meetings: "They're probably upset with me 'cause I've been missin' a few meetings. So, but I'm the treasurer of the SCLC. . . . I haven't been to a meeting in a while." Thus, while religious leaders were often part of black-centered civic organizations "on paper," they were not deeply involved and generally did not view those organizations as their primary vehicle for civic engagement. Interestingly, there was often a sense of guilt and hesitancy around speaking openly about this lack of involvement.

Most black-centered civic organizations are national organizations with local chapters. Another reason given for not being involved in these organizations was that the top-down control of the national offices was not conducive to addressing the kinds of local issues they wanted to address. Mark Thompson explained, "I really wasn't enthusiastic about running [for office in the NAACP], because most of your activism has to be preapproved by the national. . . . So your ability to sort of do what I call fire-engine activism is greatly reduced. . . . There are times in which, you know, we just don't have a lot of time to really seek approval. . . . It's like, 'The building is burning now.'" Thompson spoke in his interview about mobilizing on short notice around state budget issues and local shootings. Instead of working through black-centered civic organizations with nationwide name recognition, he chose to lead an organization he helped found that was a hub for black religious leaders to coordinate with one another on what he referred to as those "fire-engine activism" issues. Several other local religious leaders reported that their work with Thompson's organization was an important part of their public lives.

Ironically, the interviews seem to indicate that part of the problem with black-centered civic organizations was that they succeeded in achieving their goals in the civil rights movement. One pastor, Leon Harper noted,

> The more we have prospered as a people, the less we have perhaps relied on entities like NAACP. Possibly to our own detriment, we have taken it for granted. Because a lot of what was fought for when I was a child I stand in and I'm nurtured from now. You know, the very gains that they were shooting for in that day or targets they were trying to hit, I'm a recipient of that. I can live wherever I want to live.

Because many of the goals of the civil rights movement have been achieved, and some black people have been able to achieve middle-class status as a result, there is less urgency. Indeed, individuals with a college education are more likely to attend church on a weekly basis (Pew Research Center 2017), so many of the people in the pews as well as the religious leaders are sufficiently comfortable and thus perhaps not interested in spending significant time and energy on activism. Reginald Baker shared this sentiment. He discussed the difficulty of getting middle-class people to be civically engaged: "We don't have as much pain as in the 1960s. . . . We shared a common pain that made us do what we had to, to work it out. It seems as if the more comfortable we become, the much less confrontational we become. Forget having middle-class folks involved in any kind of confrontation [*laughs*]." Leaders in mobilization efforts must be willing to engage in conflict through actions like protesting, testifying before legislators, and doing the difficult and often confrontational work of agitating people in their own community to take action. Middle-class people arguably have less motivation and urgency around these activities because of their relatively comfortable lives.

Furthermore, because of the success of the civil rights movement, organizations like the NAACP are well known, and their leaders have access to power in local institutions. A few religious leaders described black-centered civic organizations as being "in the room" or "at the table," which is ostensibly the goal of many social movement organizations, to have a seat at tables of power. Edward Quincy, who was a leader with the NAACP in Cleveland, described this work in this way: "We deal with things that happen in the city. . . . Sit at the table and reason with the powers that be. Then, if not, then you figure out what else to do: boycott, picket, whatever." The interviewer followed up, asking if the NAACP had taken any action like this, and Quincy responded by saying, "No. . . . We usually resolve it at the table." Thus, black-centered civic organizations have gained prestige and recognition and enjoy a seat at the table. At the same time, they are not very active and struggle to stay relevant in a context where the gains of the civil rights movement have been institutionalized. This is an example of what happens when a social movement organization achieves its goals and does not reorient itself to achieving new goals (e.g., challenging the criminal justice system). It is also an example of how effective hegemonies work. They incorporate leaders of counterhegemonic movements in the structure (or at the table). This, over time, diffuses counterhegemonic movements' power.[1]

In sum, our interviews indicate that black-centered civic organizations were not a major hub for social mobilization in Ohio cities. While these organizations were well suited to push for the goals of the civil rights movement, once they achieved their aims, they did not evolve and revitalize their approach. Instead, they became part of existing institutions, claimed a seat at the table, and ossified. Therefore, in the era of post-civil-rights-era racism (Bobo, Kluegel, and Smith 1996; Dovidio and Gaertner 2004; Bonilla-Silva 2001), black-centered civic organizations did not inspire black religious leaders or provide a robust vehicle for social change. Given this disconnect between black-centered civic organizations and the social mobilization needs of black communities, what role do FBCO coalitions play in filling the gap?

Faith-Based Community Organizing

Faith-based community organizing is a field of organizations that mobilizes churches and other faith communities to push for social change. FBCOs are coalitions of churches that are based in cities and affiliated with regional or national networks. A faith community can become a "member" of an FBCO coalition by paying dues and collaborating with FBCO community organizers to train leaders in their congregations to participate in issue campaigns. FBCOs can provide member churches with significant resources for mobilization, including paid staff who provide political education and training in leadership and organizing skills for congregation members. They can also connect religious leaders to nationwide social networks that include relationships with prominent clergy, funders, academics, and political operatives. FBCO coalitions work on a variety of economic and racial justice issues, including access to affordable housing and public transit, police accountability, predatory lending, health care, immigration reform, and educational equity. They use a variety of tactics, including protest, to achieve their goals. Still, their aims are not black-centered.

FBCOs and Race

FBCO coalitions are often multiracial. Richard Wood and Brad Fulton (2015) describe how FBCO coalitions are significantly more diverse than other civic institutions in the United States and thus provide an important space for building social capital across race. However, they also found in a 2011 national survey that racial diversity in FBCO coalitions had declined over the previous decade, and the percentage of majority-white institutions had increased. Wood and Fulton point to the way FBCOs' strategic decisions—as well as structural social trends, including declining black congregations and economic adversity in urban cores—have contributed to the whitening of the field. Many coalitions have increased religious diversity by bringing in more predominantly white institutions, like Unitarian Universalists, and by expanding into whiter areas, like the suburbs. In 1999, 35 percent of FBCO-member faith communities were predominantly black. In 2011, the percentage had decreased to 30 percent. Faith communities of color were more likely to leave FBCO coalitions. Of these, black member churches were least likely to be replaced by another black member faith community. Wood and Fulton do not account for why black churches leave FBCO coalitions. Our conversations with black religious leaders in Ohio reveal that there are several factors at play in black churches' decisions to disaffiliate from FBCOs.

Historically, FBCO networks and coalitions have preferred a "color-blind" or "race neutral" approach to organizing. This was an intentional strategy that was promoted to unite people across race on common issues. In recent years, this strategy has been changing, largely due to consistent criticism from people of color. Many FBCO coalitions and networks are now explicit and intentional about addressing race and formally incorporate a racial equity framework into their organizational training and practices. Wood and Fulton (2015) describe how this change has taken place across the field. However, this change has been uneven, and local conditions vary greatly.

Even in contexts where white leaders are explicit about addressing racial inequity, the fact remains that the organizations are heavily influenced by predominantly white funders. Organizations compete with one another for short-term grants, and to be successful, they must match their organization's agenda to goals that funders want to pursue. Then, funders hold organizations accountable through regular reports and check-ins. The second author has outlined elsewhere how this dynamic deeply distorts movements because organizations are fundamentally accountable to elites rather than to the base of people being organized (Oyakawa 2017). It is important to note that these funders do not prioritize issues that disproportionately impact black people, like mass incarceration and police brutality against people of color, opting to instead support nonpartisan civic engagement and advocacy on issues like health care (Oyakawa 2017). This lack of attention to issues specific to black communities changed somewhat after the first round of Black Lives Matter protests in 2014–15, but even that shift serves to underscore how the funders who help shape the agendas for nonprofit organizations are responding to social movements, not leading them. Thus, while black religious leaders tend to agree with the political agenda of FBCOs, the broad-based rhetoric of these multiracial organizations and their tendency to focus on issues of interest to white elites mean that black pastors do not always experience FBCOs as a vehicle for them to lead on issues of particular importance to the black community.

Black Religious Leaders' Involvement in FBCOs

Still, many of the religious leaders in our sample described involvement with FBCOs. Why would black religious leaders choose to work with these organizations instead of black-centered civic organizations? One reason is that they saw the utility of community-organizing methods and having support from professional organizing staff. Reginald Baker was a typical pastor in our study. He was once very involved in an FBCO organization but had eventually backed away. Reflecting on his prior experience with the FBCO, he said,

> I mean, so, I might be up here talking in front of the meeting, but, "How did you get all these people to the meeting?" We had staff that built relationships and called these people fifty times trying to get them all here. And it's a heck of a lot of work that goes on behind the scenes; but, for most of our organizations, we don't have staff dedicated to the outreach, collaboration-building-type piece.

Baker saw the value of the FBCO model for organizing and community mobilization, and later in his interview, he noted that black-centered civic organizations lack the financial resources to support organizing staff. Upon reflecting further on other black churches' involvement with FBCOs, he said, "Some of them are getting involved just because of the vision of that interracial, multicultural-type stuff. Some are getting involved because it's the best thing around, because, as much as we would like to have these black coalitions, it don't look like it's happening anytime soon or it's not strong enough, so they jump on that." Most of the religious leaders who spoke about FBCOs drew a sharp distinction between multiracial coalitions and black coalitions that focus on black issues. In this pastor's mind, being a part of a multiracial coalition was attractive for some black religious leaders, but for him, the ideal would be to have a black coalition. However, that possibility seemed unlikely in his local context. Black religious leaders, in his view, worked with a multiracial FBCO because it was "the best thing around" and provided resources like organizing staff who could help build relationships and pull off large public meetings.

Black religious leaders, if involved in an FBCO, generally chose to do so because they perceived it as the best organizing gig around. Preferably, they would have a way to organize for issues salient to black communities, which FBCOs do not center. What does it look like, then, for black religious leaders to be involved in these organizations? How do they manage this tension? In the following sections, we explore these questions, discussing black religious leaders' involvement with FBCOs in three Ohio cities.

Three Cities, Three Different Organizational Contexts

FBCOs vary significantly based on their (1) national network and (2) local leadership. While we interviewed religious leaders in smaller cities and towns, the vast majority were affiliated with religious organizations in the three largest cities in the state: Cleveland, Columbus, and Cincinnati. This allowed us to account for different organizational contexts across the state from the perspectives of black religious leaders and civic leaders. It is also important to look at these cities separately because each of the FBCOs in the three major cities is affiliated with different national FBCO networks. This is important because, historically, organizations from different national FBCO networks have been competitive, even hostile with one another, in part because of heavy competition for funding (Hall and Hall 1996; Warren and Wood 2001). Each of these organizations thus uses a slightly different organizing method, and the leaders of these organizations for the most part do not coordinate with one another; instead, they primarily coordinate with others in their regional and national networks.

Additionally, FBCO organizations are often unstable community institutions. The history of an FBCO in any given city is likely to include starts and stops. Sometimes there was an organizer who was not a good fit. Or a split emerged over a particular issue during the course of trying to organize, leading the FBCO to atrophy. When this happens, sometimes FBCO organizing is revived later under new leadership and perhaps a new name. We saw these patterns with the FBCO organizations in Ohio. At the time of this study, the FBCO organizations across Cleveland, Columbus, and Cincinnati were in different phases of development, renewal, and relationship building with black religious leaders in the city. To capture how this variation may have mattered for black religious leaders' engagement in FBCOs, we organize the remainder of our analysis by city.

Cleveland: Hopeful Beginnings

In Cleveland, our interviews with black religious leaders did not reveal a strong memory of FBCO organizing in the region.[2] There was a brand-new FBCO getting off the ground. An Industrial Areas Foundation (IAF) organizer who arrived the year prior to our study worked with local clergy to establish a new organization called Greater Cleveland Congregations (GCC). This organization featured prominently in several of our interviews with clergy, who reported deep involvement. Given the nationwide trends discussed earlier, it is an open question whether GCC will be able to sustain black clergy involvement over the long run. However, our interviews point to effective leadership on the part of the lead organizer, who was able at the time to draw religious leaders into the organization. Those whom we spoke with expressed satisfaction with their experiences in the organization.

Religious leaders who were newly involved with the FBCO in Cleveland explained that they were drawn to the organization's approach to doing politics and the community-organizing model. Peter Mills, whom you will meet more extensively in chapter 6, was a relatively young, influential pastor in Cleveland. He described what attracted him to be part of GCC:

> The community-organizing model simply, you know, looks at not only . . . the traditional leaders within a congregation, i.e., the pastor or, you know, the clergy, ministers, and what have you, but it also looks at the people within the congregation and in large mass using their numbers to be able to affect change. . . . We have found that there's a great amount of power and influence when we kind of work in coalition. And it's actually been quite successful.

Mills was excited by the potential for leveraging his sizable congregation to exercise power and influence over issues that he cares about. FBCO organizations provided resources to train lay leaders in congregations how to organize. Because of this, Mills saw GCC as a means to help him mobilize his congregation on issues that he cared about, such as criminal justice reform. Furthermore, the organization was useful, in his view, because it expanded the coalition's ability to exercise power.

The FBCO approach attracts religious leaders not only because of the methodology for training congregational leaders but also because of the types and breadth of issues they work on, with the goal of impacting the social causes of community problems. For instance, when Gary Crawford was asked about why he was involved with Greater Cleveland Congregations, he said, "It's because GCC looks at structural changes. . . . It doesn't look to respond to, you know, whatever issue is pressing at the moment, but it looks at structural issues and how we can impact those structural issues for long-term impact on a large number of people. . . . One of our big issues right now is Medicaid expansion." For religious leaders who want to work on policy change and antipoverty initiatives that have the potential to impact many people, community organizing can be an appealing option.

Crawford's involvement with GCC was particularly notable because he was hesitant to get involved. He had a bad experience with an FBCO in another city, so GCC's lead organizer had to convince him to give it another chance. He explained,

> There's a similar group sponsored by a different organization when I was pastoring in [another city]. And I was on board with the goals of the organizations but had a bad experience with the organizer there. . . . My hesitation has to do with a past bad experience with a personality as opposed to with the concept. I was on board with the concept, just proceeded cautiously in terms of looking at who was going to be involved, particularly on the institutional end.

Crawford's past experience with the FBCO was not uncommon. Others shared having negative experiences with FBCOs related to specific organizers or leaders whose style or tactics they did not agree with. This often created a formidable obstacle for any organizer who wanted to engage clergy in an area where other FBCOs generated bad feelings toward FBCOs. However, the lead organizer of GCC was able to convince Crawford that he would have a better experience in Cleveland.

This paid dividends for GCC. Crawford ended up becoming very engaged with the organization. He explained,

> I've been very involved particularly with Greater Cleveland Congregations. So in any given week, I'm normally doing something that has something to do with the work in that area. . . . There's always something going on. . . . For instance, just yesterday, we met with the—the CEO of the Cleveland Schools. . . . Greater Cleveland Congregations was involved in the—in the Levy Campaign in Cleveland. And now we're just doing our follow-up work, in terms of—of how this transformation plan and the transformation alliance, how that—that whole piece is going to work. So, um, we met with the CEO and the mayor's chief person on education to talk about going forward, how the money's going to be spent, and so forth.

Thus, Crawford was contributing a significant amount of his time and energy to the issues and causes that GCC pursued on a regular basis, to the point where he was participating in GCC-related activities on a weekly basis. This work ended up putting him in contact with influential city leaders. One of GCCs first mobilization campaigns was to get a school funding levy passed. When it did, the black religious leaders who worked with GCC on the campaign got access to "the table" and the opportunity to influence how the money would be spent. Crawford viewed GCC as an effective way to impact local politics and found working with GCC rewarding.

It is important to remember that GCC was established in 2011, and our interviews took place in 2012, when the organization was still fairly new. News coverage in early 2020 indicated that GCC was still active and continuing to mobilize significant numbers of clergy and lay leaders. But there were signs that maintaining the coalition had not been easy work. In 2017, for instance, two black churches and two synagogues announced that they would be leaving the organization over a disagreement about one of GCC's issue campaigns, objecting to a large investment in a sports venue. The dispute was covered by local news media (Bamworth 2017).

Still, GCC continues to maintain the support of prominent local black pastors, according to the organization's website. This is not the norm. As we will see in the following sections, several black religious leaders in Cincinnati and Columbus were very engaged with a local FBCO early on in their pastoral careers but later discontinued their involvement for various reasons.

Cincinnati: Change Is the Only Constant

In Cincinnati, the FBCO in 2012 was the Amos Project. The Amos Project maintained a presence in the city since the early 2000s and was affiliated with a statewide coalition called the Ohio Organizing Collaborative (OOC) and the PICO national network (now Faith in Action). At the time of our interviews, the Amos Project had just undergone a leadership transition and was in a rebuilding phase.

The history of FBCOs in Cincinnati included a predecessor organization to Amos in the 1990s called United Churches Active in Neighborhoods (UCAN). The first paid organizer of UCAN was a black pastor in our sample. He described the community-organizing methods he employed in the 1990s as well as how his views evolved over time:

> [You] find out what the needs are and get people fired up—um, do what's called an "action." You know find out who's not doing what they should be doing, bring them to a meeting of about five hundred angry people, sit them in a chair all by themselves, and then yes or no questions. . . . And you . . . you start to win victories. You start with small, winnable victories—you know, trash collection, overgrown weeds on stairs, whatever it is the community's seein'. You know, "We need a stop sign." And . . . then that works, and it's powerful, especially on smaller issues. As you get larger, it kind of . . . it tends to break apart. It's always only based on, you know, the needs of a community and the anger of a community. And the question becomes at the end of the day, Does it really build and strengthen community? . . . I like both. . . . Let's fight with both hands, not just the hand of our needs and our anger. But also let's build community based on what we already have existing to build something sustainable. . . . Hence the asset-based community building. So I galvanize more towards that.

This pastor critiques the community-organizing methodology he utilized in the 1990s for being too focused on addressing community anger and immediate needs without building community unity and strength. He subsequently moved away from the FBCO to other models of action that focus on building assets for the black community. He was not a member of the Amos Project in 2012.[3]

Conrad Stevenson was also involved in this FBCO. He was even president of the organization at one point. But he discontinued his involvement over theological differences with other members of the coalition:

> It was a good group. But then, when it became a little different, we pulled out. Because . . . all churches don't believe the same thing. . . . I think the thing that kind of broke the camel's back was when a person got up and prayed and, uh, and just kept referring to God as "She," and the members were like, "Ohh." I don't know if you were there that day. But the members were like, "President, you know, God ain't no she." And so it was like, "Reverend, I don't know if we want to be a part of this anymore." You know, and so we kind of pulled away from it.

Black Protestants tend to be theologically conservative, as we discussed, and thus do not always appreciate being exposed to the beliefs and practices of more liberal denominations that are often part of FBCO coalitions. Because FBCO events often involve shared prayer and worship, these differences in belief can be a significant obstacle to their continued participation. In this case, the theological differences proved too much, and Stevenson withdrew his church from the organization.

Just as there is constant change in the field of FBCOs, black religious leaders' relationships with FBCOs are ever evolving. It is not uncommon for a rebranding to take place when an FBCO coalition falls apart. The Amos Project was birthed from the remnants of UCAN. Stevenson, who just described disaffiliating from the FBCO in the 1990s, also described working with the Amos Project in 2012 for a voter-mobilization event. The Amos Project, along with other partners like the Urban League and Ohio Unity Coalition, provided a tent, food, and organizing staff to conduct voter-registration training at Stevenson's church. His church provided the meeting space and turned out volunteer leaders from the congregation who attended the training and spent the afternoon registering people to vote. Participation in FBCO activities is thus somewhat fluid. While Stevenson intentionally disaffiliated from UCAN and was not a member of the Amos Project, he was willing to partner with and contribute resources to joint activities with the Amos Project under certain circumstances, namely, get-out-the-vote efforts.

A common refrain among religious leaders who lessened or discontinued their involvement with FBCOs was that they could not commit the time necessary for the endeavor. Baker had been involved with an FBCO organization in another city but was not involved with the Amos Project in Cincinnati. He explained,

> Just don't have the time and energy. I would be supportive of my members getting involved. And I would promote the events and talk it up. But I find myself just trying to really be strategic, uh, with time and energy. . . . It's just a lot of meetings. . . . I would encourage my members to go get involved and be a liaison between our church and this organization. And, you know, I give you prime time to talk up what you're trying to do. If you need a few dollars, I can help you do that. But me personally going to all of those meetings, it just don't fit anymore. . . . I used to do that.

Involvement in an FBCO generally entails going to a lot of meetings. Because these organizations are often working on multiple issue campaigns at once, the work can take up a significant proportion of religious leaders' time if they do not set strict boundaries. So while this pastor supported the mission and work of the FBCO, he was no longer willing to prioritize attending FBCO meetings.

FBCO coalitions can provide a vehicle for black churches to have a voice in local issues, and the Amos Project in Cincinnati did experience some success in engaging black religious leaders in this work. Campbell described what this looked like when he worked with the Amos Project to ensure that a local development project would provide jobs for African Americans:

> Our organization, Amos Project, decided to pull together some allies. We had approached county and city leaders about it. They refused to act. So we had . . . a public gathering, a major press event where we actually

presented the issues to the community as a whole, that this is really what's happening underneath the surface, you know. . . . We had county officials and city officials that finally showed up when we forced the issue out into the public light. . . . And from that meeting forward, now there was a greater sense of urgency and a greater sense—a greater desire—to hear and understand what the community was asking for, and immediately change began to happen. . . . The committee that was making all the decisions was an all-white committee. . . . We were able to get eventually . . . two African Americans were actually placed on the committee.

This description was typical of FBCO campaigns with regard to their mobilization tactics. The main tactic that FBCO organizations use is a public meeting, bringing together a large number of citizens with public officials to hold them accountable to address the community's needs. The leaders agitate and negotiate for greater representation in decision-making bodies or a concrete shift on an issue of interest or both. Note that Campbell viewed the Amos Project as "our organization"; this kind of ownership indicates that there was probably a relationship of trust between this pastor and the organizing staff.

FBCO actions can yield mixed results, and communities do not always get what they want. Campbell reflected on the campaign just described, saying,

We didn't get, in the end, what we were pushing for. But what it did was it raised the issue, and it got more churches and more religious leaders informed and connected with efforts like the Amos Project and concerned about these social issues and realizing that we have a responsibility to be informed and to be engaged and to make sure that we take advantage of the rights that we have as citizens. . . . Religious leaders and churches now are much more typically civically engaged than ever before. The members are as well. And it's important that that continues, because that shows that the church is relevant.

There are several important things to note about this quote. First, the campaign was ultimately unsuccessful in achieving its aims. Thus, a significant amount of time and energy was put into an endeavor that did not yield the desired result. Campbell finds a silver lining, however, in how leadership development, education, and the practice of taking action together helped build community capacity for political action and make the church relevant in the world.

Ultimately, the goal of community organizing is to empower ordinary people, and it is a long-term endeavor. In fact, Campbell's takeaway from this campaign was not dissimilar to McCormick's assertion earlier about the need to build community. The successful actions of the civil rights movement were preceded by decades of community and institution building, and even then there were many campaigns that failed to achieve their primary aims. It takes time to build enough power to truly make an impact, and some issues are more winnable than others (McAdam 1982). Thus, even if a particular campaign is not successful, participating in an FBCO can help churches develop leaders and strengthen social networks; these are resources that can be utilized for future mobilization.

In summary, the FBCO in Cincinnati had been uneven, with stops and starts and consistent turnover in leadership. There was constant activity, however, and black religious leaders moved in and out of the organizing work as it fit their needs and schedules. The Amos Project did not emerge as a central hub for organizing black religious leaders, but the organization had a positive reputation among most of our interviewees.

Columbus: Stability and Attrition

In Columbus, the FBCO was BREAD, which is affiliated with Direct Action Research and Training Center (DART). The DART organizing model was somewhat different from that of GCC and the Amos Project. BREAD's work followed the same pattern each year, starting with a listening campaign and house meetings, followed by a vote that decided three issues that the entire organization would focus on that year, culminating in a large public meeting with several thousand people to hold public officials accountable to the organization's agenda. This structure was fairly rigid, with the same process every year. The intention was to ensure that the organization remained democratic and accountable to the grassroots. More fluid organizations, like the Amos Project, did not have members vote on all the issues the organization worked on. BREAD was established in the mid-'90s and in 2012 had had the same leadership for over sixteen years. Our study included several religious leaders who had been involved in BREAD in the past but were no longer part of the organization.

While most religious leaders were reluctant to openly denounce any organization and often hedged any critiques with ambiguous language or faint praise, Rick Richardson was unusually forthright in his criticism of BREAD. We did not have to read between the lines to decipher his meaning. For him, a major issue was that the organization was predominantly white, particularly with regard to its staff:

> When BREAD first started, most of your significant African American churches were a part of it, supported it financially. . . . Within two years, we saw it. We saw it very clearly. We saw the fact that they were bringing in these folks who didn't look like us to run this, to tell us how they thought we ought to do this. And we're like, "Are you serious?" And it usually was a young, white male who had some experience somewhere else. And Columbus is different. I tell people this all the time. I've lived in other cities. Columbus is different. What works in other cities doesn't work here.

Richardson did not appreciate that the young, white organizers employed by DART believed that they were the experts in how to mobilize his community. This suggests a problem with paternalism in FBCOs, where tactics developed by and for white institutions are assumed to be the most effective organizing methods universally. The organizers' insistence on following the existing DART organizing model meant that Richardson's deep knowledge of the local context was not taken into account. The organization's lack of flexibility communicated a lack of respect, which was not conducive to building trust.

Not only did Richardson take exception to the organizing model, but he also found that he felt more solidarity with the public officials who were the targets of BREAD actions than with the organization itself. He continued,

> I question BREAD's tactics: the bullying, the—the forcing, you know. And if you come to a BREAD meeting, the primary folks sitting in BREAD are white, suburban folks who come in and want to say, "This is what's best in

this community." . . . And most of the politicians I felt they were beating up looked like me and you. . . . So I'm like, "I'm not going to be privy. I've got access to them. I don't need y'all to get me access to any of these folks." So anything I need to say to [the mayor] or whatever the case may be . . . BREAD is still out there, and I tell [public officials], . . . I said, "BREAD is a shadow. Y'all just ain't figured that out. Ain't no substance to it." They give the appearance of power. I said, "But if you survey that crowd and say, 'How many of y'all live in Columbus and can vote?' Not too many of them." Not too many. . . . There are very few large African American churches that are part of BREAD.

From Richardson's perspective, BREAD was a predominantly white, suburban organization that was trying to exercise influence in the city. He did not need to go through this organization to influence public officials or access the resources that he wanted to. He asserted that BREAD lacked power because it did not have enough Columbus voters and African American churches to truly pose a threat to the leaders it wanted to hold accountable.

While other Columbus pastors were not as direct in their statements about BREAD as Richardson was, several interviewees seemed to share Richardson's evaluation that it was not the right vehicle for black pastors and churches to have their voices heard. Jackson Smith struck a softer tone and seemed reluctant to openly criticize the organization, yet the basic gist of his narrative was similar to Richardson's:

I feel bad that I don't work with them anymore. . . . Good organization. I'm telling you, when we first started, whew, it was a—it was a force. It was a force, because really we had—it was black, white, urban, suburban, Protestant, Catholic, and Jews. . . . Then, as your victories happen, you, of necessity, have to change. . . . When you walk in the boardroom—see, when you get in the boardroom, you've got to take off your brogan boots and put on some slip-ons. I mean, what you wore to kick the door in may not need to be what you wear once you get to the table.

When BREAD was a new organization, there was excitement about the coalition, and "it was a force." Smith then alluded to black religious leaders in Columbus since gaining access to the halls of power in the city.

It did not make sense, from his perspective, to use the often confrontational tactics that BREAD promoted, which placed the organization and its constituency outside the halls of power. Instead, he preferred to pursue an insider strategy that was less confrontational.

Similarly, Darryl Kane was not involved with BREAD anymore in part because he found the organization to be ineffective. He said,

> The people who were involved—of all persuasions, denominations, faiths, races—they weren't very influential people. So the influence of course came with the numbers, as with any community-organizing organization, but still limited in terms of capacity and what they could really accomplish or what they could put the spotlight on some things in terms of really doing some things. . . . Decisions are being made on the golf course and, you know, in the governor's mansion and other places. You know, it didn't go far.

Kane expressed dissatisfaction with BREAD particularly with the limited influence the organization brought to bear. He noted that elites made decisions without regard for noninfluential people. A large public gathering did not necessarily change this. There is truth to this criticism, especially in light of the preceding accounts. Given the standpoint of black religious leaders in Columbus and their position as respected community leaders with significant influence over local politicians' electoral base, it makes sense that they strategically focused on building relationships with black elected officials and exercising influence through their access to those officials.

Finally, Herman Wilson told a familiar narrative about being part of the organization for a limited time and then discontinuing after a fairly short period once he realized that the organization was not helping him achieve his goals:

> When I first became pastor my first year, my first year or first two years, I participated in BREAD, . . . went to their meetings, really kind of got involved and went to their final big meeting. . . . I was involved for—for a year or two, and then I stopped. . . . I just felt like that the process was very consuming, time-consuming. . . . I was not ready to give everything that they were asking. The BREAD group has a purpose and issue, a defi-

nite, you know, reason why they're, you know, doing what they're doing. That was the major reason why I said, "Okay, this is—this is not in line with my goals and vision as pastor. I have to figure out other ways to give back to the community and invest in community issues."

The organizing process that BREAD followed each year placed significant time demands on leaders. Wilson ultimately found that working with BREAD was not helping him advance his own agenda and therefore decided it was best to part ways and pursue other ventures.

Black religious leaders in Columbus decided to pursue an insider strategy utilizing their connections with city officials instead of the outsider strategy favored by FBCO organizations like BREAD. They believed that they could exercise more influence that way. Furthermore, they wanted to have control over the agenda. The democratic process of BREAD's organizing model did not allow them to pursue their own issues. The process that BREAD asked churches to submit to meant that black religious leaders ended up spending time and resources on issues that might not be relevant to their own goals or the communities they represented. This did not sit well with several of the black religious leaders in this study.

We can contrast these accounts from Columbus with the story told earlier by Crawford from Cleveland, who viewed GCC as a useful vehicle that put him in rooms with powerful people to negotiate and work on issues that mattered to him. The Columbus stories were also distinct from that of Campbell from Cincinnati, who framed his involvement with the Amos Project in terms of how his church's work with the FBCO increased black religious leaders' political capacity and awareness of local issues. So even when black religious leaders were unable to "win" on their issue, the experience was valuable for building community over the long term. Clearly, black clergy had a variety of experiences with FBCOs. Some contributing factors were differences in organizing methods, leadership, and local context. It remains to be seen, however, whether the FBCO model can make a meaningful, lasting impact on core issues like the poverty and criminalization plaguing black neighborhoods and the systemic murders of unarmed black people. While FBCO methods have proven to win local victories in some cases, it is reasonable to question whether they are undoing white supremacy and accomplishing the level of structural change required to achieve true freedom for blacks and other people of color in the United States.

* * *

Organizations are important for sharing resources and coordinating with others for mobilization around social issues. In three Ohio cities where we interviewed leaders in 2012, black-centered civic organizations were, for the most part, understood to be anemic and did not have wide appeal as vehicles for action among black religious leaders. Faith-based community organizing offered an alternative, and there was significant involvement among the people we interviewed. However, there was not consistent investment or satisfaction with the results of organizing with FBCOs.

One benefit of working with FBCOs is access to resources such as organizing staff. Religious leaders are busy and stretched thin. Professional organizers can help with the legwork of mobilization, including building relationships with and training lay leaders in organizing and political skills, setting up meetings, and coordinating actions. In order for this model to work, however, it is crucial for there to be a relationship of strong trust between the organizer and pastor. Where this breaks down, it is difficult for an organization to be effective, and there is attrition, often with hard feelings that can make it more difficult for another organization or leader to cultivate the necessary trust. But in instances when the model works, FBCOs can be a vehicle for religious leaders to address community issues in coalition with other churches, build political capacity within their congregations, and expand their own power and influence.

There were several factors that made it more difficult to build trusting relationships between organizers and religious leaders. First and foremost, FBCOs are often led and controlled by white people. People of color are leaders in these organizations. But there is evidence that white professionals have an easier time accessing resources like foundation grants that allow them to hire dedicated organizing staff (Oyakawa 2017). This pattern is seen in other multiracial religious contexts. People of color in predominantly white evangelical outreach ministries are at a disadvantage, relative to their white colleagues, at fundraising (Perry 2012). This is also true for pastors of color of multiracial churches when it comes to resources like social capital (Munn 2019) and formal authority (Edwards and Kim 2019). Further, there is often not much that people of color can do to hold FBCOs that are largely led by whites accountable to working on their core issues. This can create a dynamic whereby people of color must set aside their primary interests to work on campaigns that a multiracial coalition agrees on.[4] Issues chosen by the coalition might not be the most urgent for black communities. This problem can be exacerbated if the FBCO is inflexible and does not allow leaders to shape their involvement to suit their own needs. Some community-organizing methodologies can be rigid, unnatural, and ineffective for mobilizing communities of color, in part because they were often developed by and for white institutions. Time, energy, and money are precious resources, and if they are not being directed toward ends that religious leaders feel are advancing their constituents' or their personal and professional goals, they are likely to become disengaged. This outcome is not inevitable, but it is made more likely by the structures that religious leaders and organizers are embedded in. A successful coalition is a rare and fragile thing.

Despite the obstacles that exist, some black religious leaders have been able to advance their aims through involvement with FBCOs and are cautiously optimistic about moving forward with multiracial coalitions. However, the relationship is tenuous. Ultimately, the fact is that over the course of the twenty-plus-year history of the field, FBCOs have not been able to build enough power to contest and overcome the major structural forces that keep black communities impoverished, overpoliced, and disengaged from politics. But as one pastor stated earlier, FBCOs, not black-centered civic organizations, have often been the best option that black religious leaders can see for being engaged in public life.

6

The General, the Warrior, and the Protégé

There are some people whose voices simply matter more than others. This is not something we often openly acknowledge in our society, where a high value is placed on egalitarianism. This is particularly the case if the "mattering" is based on informal qualities, like charisma or connections. Yet the reality remains that some people matter more than others, for a community's direction, vitality, culture, and future. Certain people have more influence than others. Their ideas are perceived to matter more. Their values, beliefs, and behaviors are seen as ones to be emulated. And they are situated in highly advantageous locations in their community's social network, ones that connect them to other people who matter and people who have valuable resources. All this allows them to guide and energize their community in critical ways.

Several people in the Ohio black religious leader network stand out among their peers as people who matter. We highlight three because they count in distinct and particular ways. They are from different generations. And while they have varying yet (mostly) complementary views about social engagement and theology, they each satisfy certain, unique roles in the network, roles that no other person in the study filled. We refer to these people as the General, the Warrior, and the Protégé. These names are chosen to reflect their main role in the Ohio black religious network. One of them is also a principal leader, Wyoming Brashear, whom you were introduced to in chapter 3.

We more intimately introduce you to these key people in the Ohio black religious leader network by providing abridged versions of their interviews. We have eliminated text that is redundant or verbose. We privilege their views and experiences related to mobilization and social matters. These are their words, views, experiences, and explanations for what they do. Collectively, their stories offer a glimpse into where the black church has been, where it has attempted to go, and where it may be headed in the future.

The General

I (the lead author) had been playing phone tag with Brashear for several weeks when I finally got in touch with him. After brief niceties, he explained that he was actually in my city for a speaking engagement. I was excited to learn this. I jumped at the chance to meet with him while he was nearby. I asked him on that phone call if he could meet with me later that evening. To my surprise, he agreed.

I met Brashear at the hotel where he was staying. The plan was to have the interview conversation over dinner since it was to take place during the evening. I waited for Brashear in the hotel lobby. I did not know what he looked like, but when I saw a tall, thin, African American man come from the elevator banks dressed in a light-colored suit and expressing a smooth, gracious demeanor, I knew right away it was Brashear. This was in part because we were in a part of the city where there were few black people. But it was also how one could imagine him to look after hearing how his peers described him.

My initial impression was confirmed in the interview. I, admittedly, came to be a little in awe of him myself as the interview progressed. I found him to be kind, respectful, and gracious. I left very appreciative of the opportunity to share just a bit of time with this "icon."

The Interview

INTERVIEWER: Do you think pastors should be involved in civic activity?

BRASHEAR: I think pastors are morally, spiritually, and personally obligated to be involved in civic affairs . . . and in the total life of the community and the nation. . . . I see that as a part of our calling. . . . And I think that that calling is biblically anchored. . . . And if I were to use a specific reference, I would draw from the book of Isaiah, chapter 61, which is repeated by Jesus in the fourth chapter of the Gospel of Luke, when he read from the book of Isaiah in the synagogue at Azreth, which says, "The Spirit of the Lord is upon me. Because he hath anointed me to preach the Gospel to the poor to open the eyes of the blind, to set captives free to set at liberty who are bruised and proclaim the acceptable year of the Lord; the Year of Jubilee," which is freedom. I think our calling is anchored in that biblical imperative.

I think our calling is also historically connected with the liberation emancipation movement of history. And I think we are as to Richard Allen and Frederick Douglass and Sojourner Truth, Bishop Henry McNeal Turner, Mary McLeod Bethune, Asa Philip Randolph, W. E. B. DuBois, and especially Martin Luther King Jr. And if we are to be authentic, prophetic leaders, we have to be concerned about justice, liberation, and reconciliation.

INTERVIEWER: Do you think black religious leaders are addressing [issues related to "justice, liberation, and reconciliation"] today?

BRASHEAR: Some are addressing it in a most profound way. . . . There is a new generation of men and women in ministry who are courageous, who have moral courage, and [who are] articulating and participating in the great issues of our time. . . . Now, there are some—and this has always been the case—who tend to evade, shy away from these critical issues or do not see that as a part of their calling. . . . They see their mission in a sense of evangelical, dynamic. They're helping people to get right with God. . . . But they don't necessarily see their mission of helping the community get right with justice, humanity, equality, and the value of every human being without regard to race, creed, color, or gender or gender preference.

INTERVIEWER: Do you think there's a potential for any mobilization like [the civil rights movements] today?

BRASHEAR: There is always that potential, but there's a certain aspect to a revolution that's planned, and there's another aspect that grows out of moments unexpected. The *Brown v. Board of Education* case was well planned, practiced, orchestrated. And the genius of Thurgood Marshall and Charles Hamilton Houston can never be underestimated. But then there comes moments when something special happens, and it sparks a dynamic in history that changes everything.

INTERVIEWER: What could be the spark today?

BRASHEAR: Dr. King described it from time to time as an accumulation of years of indignity, humiliation, struggle, until at one point, our cup of endurance ran over and, we stood up. . . . After a while, people get tired, tired of being—[Dr. King] said, in his own unique way, "tired of being pushed out of the sunlight of life's July and forever cast into the fall of an Alpine November." And it's hard to totally plan that moment, but what we have to do is plant the seeds: teach, reach, practice, mobilize, and organize. And eventually the moment will come. We don't know when or where it will be. We might be looking for it in one place, and it breaks out in another. Nobody predicted the sit-in movement, which started at a lunch counter, but it did. And in a short while, it had swept every black college campus in the nation. And white students joined us from the North. We literally changed this nation.

INTERVIEWER: What I'm hearing you say—correct me if I'm wrong—is that any type of movement may need to be largely made up of young people?

BRASHEAR: It has to be intergenerational. . . . Now, there are some things that young people can do that nobody else can do. . . . They have the energy. They have the freedom. They are not tied down to children or grandchildren. And they are not necessarily employed as they will be. . . . So they can move from here to there. [The older generation] provides resources, knowledge—the narrative, the story, the history, and a special kind of support and counsel. But we should never attempt to stop the [younger generation's] movement because we think they're going to make mistakes. We did. [Laughs] We made hundreds of them. And we should not try to influence them to wait until it's safe to do thus and so because it's never safe to initiate change . . .

And there's a new set of pastors across the nation—men and women. And some people are still wrestling and foolishly grappling with women in ministry. [Laughs] So, while they are doing that, the world is moving on while they are trying to decide. They haven't read the scriptures, which says, "Your young men and women shall prophesy." . . . And this is where I gain hope and inspiration over what's going to happen in the next fifty years.

INTERVIEWER: What are your thoughts on President Obama's views on same-sex marriage? He came out with his views during the summer, I believe.

BRASHEAR: Upset a whole lot of religious leaders, some of whom are gay. To me, he did it with integrity and with honesty. And there are two things that people missed in his statement. He said, one,

"I respect those religious leaders, pastors, who might have a different point of view. I am not trying to pass a law or a constitutional amendment. I'm not issuing an executive order. I am simply giving my personal opinions." And, of course, his personal opinion doesn't matter, because he's president of the United States.

People became squeamish, and we had to do a lot of work to help the people to see that they should not confuse R-I-T-E-S with R-I-G-H-T-S. As the president of the United States, President Obama is not in charge of wedding ceremonies. He does have the responsibility to articulate the rights of every individual. I may not agree with your relationship, but I can never deny your right to love whoever you want to love. It might not be coherent with my theology, but I certainly should never infringe upon another person's constitutional rights or human rights because they are different. That's the greatness of what the president has done.

It's time for us to put an end to this long homophobic persecution and the hypocrisy involved in it. Pastors criticizing President Obama and they have a gay musician, directing the choir, and folks shouting. Do you understand what I'm saying?

Now, suppose you were to go to every museum in the country and take out all of the art that might've been produced by a gay person or remove from our hymn books all the songs that might've been written, composed, or directed by persons of the gay and lesbian community. What would happen to our Music Department? So, to stand up and sing a song from the pulpit written by a gay person and directed by a gay person and then become a gay basher is hypocritical. . . .

Now . . . President Obama's position caused people to reexamine their own attitudes. And we don't like to do that. It pushed some people out of their comfort zone. In years to come, if not already, he will be honored for standing up for the human rights and civil rights of every individual. . . . So, at that point, the president became a teacher . . . and a leader.

INTERVIEWER: Do you think that the role of the black religious leader has changed since the civil rights movement?

BRASHEAR: Not really. And I say that for two or three reasons. One, we have always had the theological perspective that we are called to introduce people to God through Jesus Christ as a Christian. . . .

Some people stop at that point. That's personal redemption and salvation. . . . But I think we are just as obligated to have both the vertical and horizontal in play, . . . the vertical meaning the individual's relationship with God, . . . the horizontal, our relationship with each other. . . . And I think we cannot separate the two. . . .

And it's biblical, because the . . . commandments that Jesus said were the greatest is "Love the Lord with all your heart, all your mind, all your soul, and all your strength." And—now, that's vertical. . . . "Your neighbor as yourself." . . . That's horizontal. . . . And when we do that, we create community. . . . If you only do the other, you just got self-righteous [laughs] individualism. . . . And . . . no sharing. . . . I do not believe in charity as a substitute for justice. . . . I believe in feeding the hungry, . . . in whatever way you can get them food . . . on an emergency basis. But I believe we also have to work at eliminating hunger. . . . And that involves social policy. . . . Mahatma Gandhi said, "God has provided enough for our needs but not enough for our greed." . . . So we have hungry people in the world, because some folks have so much. [Laughs] . . . And some people have so little.

Wyoming Brashear noted throughout his interview that he was active in significant historical moments like the civil rights movement, the presidential campaigns of Jesse Jackson, and the campaigns of President Barack Obama. This experience surely afforded him the luxury of hope, influence, and assuredness in his beliefs. He had hope that social change was possible because he saw it firsthand and helped produce it. He had influence because he had become embedded in the black religious leader network and rose to iconic status among his peers. Brashear knew what he believed and why he believed it. Perhaps this is the benefit of a long life: you live long enough to see the beginning and end of a thing and learn what is "right" and what is not.

Brashear stands out from others in this study because he consistently and intentionally aimed to reconcile his worldview, one that was historically and globally situated, with his Christian faith, drawing on biblical references to provide theological bases for his positions. This suggests that Brashear pondered matters, that his positions were not taken for granted. It was uncommon for the pastors in this study to reference specific Bible scriptures when explaining their social or theological views.

Brashear also stands out because he had been at the forefront of progressive social and theological engagement for decades, fighting against Jim Crow laws, supporting women in ministry, and affirming the rights of LGBTQ people. And then Brashear linked significant historical moments to the legacy of the African American experience and the struggle for freedom, naming specific people who were critical to this struggle, from Sojourner Truth to Martin Luther King Jr. It is no wonder he garnered such respect and admiration.

The Warrior

Brian McCormick is the Warrior. Several pastors and civic leaders we interviewed spoke very highly of him and considered him to be one of the most influential black religious leaders in their network. Once you hear his story, you know why. He had been taken under the wings of several highly influential local, regional, and national-level black religious leaders, ones who actively participated in marches and protests, some going back to the 1960s. In fact, one of the black leaders he leaned on for advice was Rev. Al Sharpton. Most significantly, McCormick had been a central leader in local, racialized social conflicts for more than a decade, leading one of the longest social protests in his city since the civil rights movement era.

McCormick was in many ways triumphant in the causes he led. Yet these triumphs came at a tremendous cost to him personally as he experienced significant sacrifice and pain as a result. The toll that the triumphs exacted on McCormick even seemed to manifest themselves physically. He is a big man, and his posture was slightly slouched as he sat in the seat across the table from me during the interview. His expressions ranged from somber to melancholy to slight exasperation. And I did not recall him smiling once during the interview. It was rare indeed that I found myself as emotionally impacted by an interview as I was by the one with Brian McCormick. His story evoked sadness in me. I was so touched that my eyes welled up with tears by the end of our conversation.

The Interview

McCORMICK: So in 2001, when the riots happened in [the city], [this church] was the place where people expected that there would be a meeting, there would be a rally, there would be organization. We would organize for the fight, for the struggle. So [this church] became known by people in the community as the Freedom Church. . . .

Somehow I became the unofficial leader of the movement, and at the time, I was president of something called Afro-Citizens Unite. . . . Because in—I think it was 2000—we have a jazz festival here, which . . . come[s] like every year. And that year, thirteen downtown restaurants closed their doors. And so here you have fifty thousand African Americans downtown for a festival and thirteen restaurants just closed their doors, wouldn't serve us. And this is in 2000! This is not 1940 or '50 or '60. This is the year 2000. So we formed a group called the Afro-Citizens Unite. We protested the restaurant closings. We met with the restaurant association and demanded that they never do that again, demanded sensitivity, demanded more diversity. . . .

After Afro-Citizens Unite formed, police killed two young men within twenty-four hours. So we were . . . a new grassroots organization. We were active. We were in the streets. We were makin' people mad. . . . And, well, both [of the young men] were unarmed, but they gave us these other stories as usual.

So we met with the president of the ministerial alliance and the president of the local NAACP. Both were [at least twenty years older than our organization]. And us, we were the young, crazy group. And both of them met with us and said, "Look we've been through this battle before. You take it." And we said, "Cool, we'll take it." So we went at 'em. And we did it right. We filed a class-action lawsuit against racial profiling in the city and police abuse. We were able to bring, like, I don't know, thirty cases together. We found a federal judge who was amenable to our cause. . . .

We . . . wanted a change that would be long lasting. So we did a mediated agreement. And we came up with something called a col-laborative agreement. . . . So we filed the lawsuit. We brought to the table the police union, the city, ourselves representing the black community. We brought together like thousands of voices from policemen and their wives in the community. And we hammered out five things that everybody agreed on. . . .

So those two murders of black men precipitated the lawsuit. But then, in April 2001, another young man was killed right here in this neighborhood by police. Unarmed, running from the police, and they shot and killed him. That brought the riots, the four days of rioting that took place, and I'm like the unofficial leader. I was chosen to be president of the Afro-Citizens United, and we're doin' the lawsuit.

But one day I'm sitting in my office and somebody said, "You know, you need to come out here." I said, "Okay." So I come outside, [and] there are like thousands of angry black people in the streets, mostly young. They're just angry, and, you know, it's like, "[He] has just been killed. What are we gonna do?"

So I come out to be part of the, you know, the group. And I'm in back of the group, and I just keep getting pushed to the front. Now I'm in the front of all these people. And I'm like, "Where are we going?" You know, so I don't say that to anybody, but in my mind I'm thinking to myself, "Okay, this has to stay nonviolent," you know, 'cause we did have people throwing bricks and breaking windows. You know, you're in the front of this group. What are you gonna say? Where are you gonna go? So I take them to [a nearby city park], and we hold a rally there. I had no choice but to lead.

And so at that point, we held meetings here like every day. We kept stressing, "This is how we're gonna do it. You know, we're gonna have a nonviolent movement. And if you're not on that page, then, you know, we just ask you to leave. We're gonna fight for justice for the family of [the man who was killed]." And [by] that point, we had had fifteen black men killed by police from 1995 to 2001. . . . We had a list of demands.

But we also then formed a boycott of the city. And that's what really hurt the city. And so we had a number of artists who were coming [and] who didn't come, who sided with us. We got in touch with the unions, the teachers' unions, people who had conventions scheduled here. The Progressive Baptist Convention had their national convention scheduled here. They pulled out. And they also joined us. We had national leadership join us—Ron Daniels, Al Sharpton, Harry Belafonte, Danny Glover. . . . Civil rights leaders from back in the day reached out to us. [One of them] sent me like a boatload of material, which was all helpful because this was new.

INTERVIEWER: The movement that started in 2001, has the momentum been maintained?

McCORMICK: No. We wrestled with was it a movement or a moment. . . . And I think it was both but more moment than movement. And what we tried to do was capitalize as much as we could on the moment and get as much as we could through our boycott efforts, through our lawsuit that was filed, get as much as we could and not—and this was my take on it—not march past the victories.

I had a conversation one day with Al Sharpton. He had preached here, and then we had dinner. And my question to him was, "How do we know when we obtain the victory?" Because we were hurting the city and we were making such an impact that they kept making overtures to us. You know, "What do you want? What do you want? What's it gonna take?" But I had a group of people who said, "You know, unless we get it all, we keep marching." . . .

But my thought and question was, "Okay, we're good at rejecting. You know, they're picking off our demands and making them happen. We're pleased with that. But how does this thing end with a bang and not a fizzle?" And it pretty much ended with a fizzle.

INTERVIEWER: Because?

McCORMICK: [Sighs] I don't know. I mean, . . . it was, well, it was hard. Our boycott lasted just about as long as the Montgomery bus boycott, which was about a year. And it was hard to sustain that. We were working with and against people who—you know, they had full-time jobs to do what they did. We were all volunteers. When we fought the lawsuit, we were fighting against the city. They hired as their lawyer the black guy in DC. . . . And this is just our time. We're not getting paid. We never got a dime for any of the changes we made in the city. And it just became hard to sustain it. And then you began to lose your own people, who want to go hear the Isley Brothers, you know. It's like, "Well, how long are we gonna do this?" So we got a lot of the demands met, but we weren't able to celebrate it. And I think that's the thing we miss the most, the ability to celebrate it. . . .

Later in the interview, McCormick revisits this period in his life.

MCCORMICK: I've been in the room, you know. I know the room. I've been kicked out of the room, you know. I will go to the streets. I will work with the people. I will fight against the room. I don't want to be in the room.

And I think that was a lesson that I learned, because during the time of all the upheaval a few years ago, I went into the room. I was still president of the Afro-Citizens United. We were the most powerful group right then. So we were always invited to the table.

So I got invited to the table, [with] the Urban League, NAACP, the usual list of black leaders in the [community], the well-respected black leaders, and then the Afro-Citizens United. In that room, we formed something called CORE. . . . [I and two other people] were the three chairs of CORE. We then gave [our plan] to the mayor. And so it became the mayor's commission. . . . We formed it. We're tryin' to be strategic. We gave it to the mayor. CORE had like fifty subgroups, the normal bringin' everybody together. My job was to be there as the voice for the people. The day we brought the consultant in from the [East Coast], that day somebody came and handed me a note from the mayor. It was like a little handwritten note: "You are no longer part of CORE. You are removed." Okay? Now this is a group that we formed, [we] gave to him. So he really doesn't have the power to remove me, in my mind. But my other chairs said, "Maybe it's a good thing," you know, so they could just continue to move forward. . . . So I know what it's like to be in the room. . . . The room never changes. And the room just keeps doin' the same stuff.

INTERVIEWER: What are some of—let's say [within] the past three or four years, what are the civic issues you've been involved in?

MCCORMICK: Not much in the past three or four years. . . . I took a step back. . . . There are a lot of the church people who were with me, but then it kind of weakened the church. I ended up gettin' a divorce after twenty-three years of marriage, lost a lot of friends. . . . Most of the friends I lost were from the white community, 'cause before all of this happened, I was active. It was like, "We like [him]." I'm on boards and all this stuff. . . . [But] they were frightened. They were frightened. They didn't understand. As much as they would like to think they understood, they just didn't understand why we were fighting and why we were fighting the way we fought. . . . There was a lot that I lost.

INTERVIEWER: Was it worth it?

McCORMICK: Probably. I mean, but again, when you lose your marriage, and I don't know. Yeah, I guess. I don't know. You have to try to balance it and figure it out. But it becomes worth it as life goes on. I mean, you go through a period of depression. I didn't even realize I went through a period of depression until one day somebody said, "You know, you're depressed." And when that person said it, I thought, "You're probably right."

INTERVIEWER: Do you think there are—compared to other groups— unique issues facing African Americans?

McCORMICK: The destruction of the black family. There are economic issues that, of course, the entire nation and world are facing, but they hit us harder. The dropout rate in our community, infant mortality, the violence that is plaguing our communities . . . There are issues that could galvanize us, and I think one of the problems is that we just don't have solutions. And so it becomes kind of self-defeating to go out here and attack issues, and we really have no hard, fast solutions.

INTERVIEWER: Do you think that's because there really isn't a solution?

McCORMICK: I don't think that. I think there are a number of solutions. I think we just have to do what we're doing in a different way.

INTERVIEWER: What would that be?

McCORMICK: Well, you see that would take a long conversation about asset-based community development. . . . [But the] short version is that you can't service your way out of issues in the black community. You can't make people whole by surrounding them with services and programs. And we as a black community have bought into the myth that we are just one program away from change. And if somebody would just give us another $50,000 grant, and we just do another teen pregnancy program, then the community will be made whole. So there's this idea that if you surround people with the right amount of services, they become whole. . . .

We have every social service known to humankind in this community. Yet we're considered the worst community. So obviously there's a
disconnect between servicing people and making them whole. What
we teach is that you have to look at the community from the glass
half full as opposed to the glass half empty, recognizing that the glass
is both. It is half full, and it is half empty. The half-full part of the
glass, though, represents the gifts, assets, strengths, and abilities of a
community that reside in individuals, associations, and institutions.
The emptiness, we understand that. And what we've tried to do—for,
I don't know, . . . hundreds of years—is pour into the emptiness of
people's lives by giving them all the services and whatever else we
think they need. If that worked, [this community] would be the best
community in America. . . .

So we now know it doesn't work, but why do we keep trying and
thinking one of two things: "Well, maybe we just need to coordinate
services better." So we try that. Or "Maybe we just need more services." So we say that's not the way to do it. We say that the way to do
it is to build strong, healthy communities focusing on what we have.

Brian McCormick is a generation younger than Wyoming Brashear.
Like Brashear, McCormick learned from the opportunities or, more ac-
curately, the battles that life brought his way. While Brashear was active
in key historical moments with national significance, McCormick was
the central leader of a sustained local activist "moment." Their experiences (or battles) were thus fundamentally different. While Brashear
consistently played an active role in important national moments, his
part was advisory or ancillary, at least as it relates to influence on the
decision-making process. McCormick and his activist followers were the
strategists and agitators for local-level social change. They were making
the decisions. They were at the table. They engaged in direct action that
challenged the local government and the economy, the two institutions
where the power elite or the "movers and shakers" of the city are often
found.

What McCormick and his activist partners did in his city was legendary. He was held in high esteem among not only black religious leaders
but activists as well. But being at the center of the struggle wore McCor-

mick down physically and relationally, causing him to suffer deterioration of mental health, key relationships, and social capital among white leaders in his city.

McCormick followed in the footsteps of civil rights movement leaders before him, but ultimately their steps could not lead him or his activist followers and partners to their desired victory. By 2000, the United States changed. The racism and discrimination that African Americans faced did not look like that of the Jim Crow era, when laws were racially explicit and racism was overt. Yet, despite the covertness of post-civil-rights-era structures, they are quite effective at reproducing a racial hierarchy that mirrors that of the Jim Crow era in profound ways. McCormick and his activist partners recognized this. They challenged it. But in the end, McCormick learned an invaluable lesson from what happened to him as the leader of Afro-Citizens Unite. Systemic change is hard. It is amazingly difficult to create and even more so to sustain. If you agitate the system ("the room," as he puts it) too much, you will be ousted altogether. After being evicted from "the room," McCormick assumed a new approach to social action, one that is more local and focuses on accessing the "assets" of disadvantaged people and communities rather than directly addressing and dismantling racism and racial discrimination.

In no way can one fault McCormick for assuming a more community-based, individuals-focused approach to social change. What he did for his city and endured in the process demands tremendous respect. He is only human. He sacrificed and did exceedingly more than almost every other black religious leader in this study to expose and rectify contemporary racist structures. There simply comes a time when you realize that you cannot do what you were doing, that you cannot sacrifice anymore, that you have nothing else you can give and still survive. And all humans want to survive, thrive even.

But the reality is that when those who want to generate change no longer pay attention to "the room," when the room effectively dismisses agitators, when the room remains in control of the racist structures that advantage some and disadvantage others, the room wins.

The Protégé

My first impression of Peter Mills was "this is an in-demand, busy person," an impression I mostly got from his executive assistant who was quite an effective gatekeeper to Mills and guardian of his schedule. I expressed a strong desire to interview Mills in person and a willingness to accommodate him as best I could, even though he lived close to two hundred miles from me. But, an in-person interview was not possible. This was largely attributed to his executive assistance's insistence that his schedule just could not accommodate such a meeting. So, we did the next best thing—a phone conversation.

The day we did the interview, it was Mills' day off. After learning this, I was especially grateful that he was willing to speak to me. He was actually on his cell phone, out running errands, at least during part of our conversation. Yet, despite doing errands, Mills was engaged in the interview. He listened carefully and, as you will see, provided rather thorough responses.

Mills is a generation younger than McCormick and nearly two generations younger than Brashear. Similar to several other high status black religious leaders, he was an alumnus of an HBCU and had a graduate degree. Mills' own story combined with the ways in which older high status leaders in the sample (Brashear included) spoke of him, led me to believe he was perceived to be the future of the black religious leader network in Ohio and perhaps beyond.

Brashear said during our interview that Mills was one of the leading black religious leaders of our day, explaining that Mills was one of "a new generation of men and women in ministry . . . who have moral courage and are articulating and participating in the great issues of our time." Prominent black religious leaders like Jesse Jackson and Al Sharpton may agree with these sentiments. They both spoke at Mills' church. This at least suggests that Mills is well networked among black religious leaders nationally. Moreover, Mills is often mentioned in his city's local newspaper. He was also recognized one year as one of the top 100 African Americans who are "beginning to shape our nation's future today" by a national black media outlet.

Even though Mills has garnered considerable support and attention from the right people within black American circles, his religious and social philosophies are still in formation. This becomes more clear when they are juxtaposed with those of Brashear and McCormick. Mills' philosophies are more theoretical, not yet forged and tested by struggle and experience. The length of his path is yet ahead of him. And he is still negotiating, perhaps even with himself, what his role as a black religious leader in the twenty-first century ought to be.

The Interview

INTERVIEWER: Do you think that it's especially important for pastors of black congregations to encourage their members to participate in civic and social issues?

MILLS: Well, I think so. I think, one, historically, when you look across the spectrum of African American churches, . . . what you find was African American churches have always been engaged in trying to meet the needs of their tithers, and sometimes that meant addressing institutional powers. Sometimes that meant providing social welfare and some type of social safety net for their congregation when government resources weren't available or sufficient. So I think that there's a tradition in the black church where you are on the spectrum of looking at the needs of one's community and responding to that.

Now, the degree to which a minister may do that . . . reflects his own religious reality or his religious worldview. But I think there's always been . . . a stream with the African-American church tradition of not simply being about high in the sky, the hereafter, or it being totally evangelical, but certainly having a degree of social engagement.

I think part of that is not just social, historical, but I think it's the present social reality that we live in. I mean, when you think about [this city], 40 percent of African Americans are in poverty or 40 percent of the residents . . . are in poverty. The majority of the residents of [this city] are African Americans. One out of every three households in Ohio are on some form of social welfare. One out of every five African Americans in Ohio who are working age is unemployed. That's twice as large as the national average and almost five to seven points higher than the national average for African Americans.

I mean, for me, I think that it's really incumbent upon us, if we're seeing people in our congregation Sunday after Sunday who are adversely affected by the socioeconomic challenges of the times—it's just incumbent upon us as organizers, as community leaders, to keep in order the sense of religious responsibility to be engaged in that.

INTERVIEWER: I understand that one of the ways in which you are engaged is through a [local FBCO]. How do you address the kind of issues that you talked about via the FBCO?

MILLS: Well, we operate through community organizers, and that's actually one of the dynamics of the FBCO that really attracted me. The community-organizing model simply looks at not only the leaders within a congregation, the traditional leaders within a congregation, i.e., the pastor or the clergy, ministers, and what have you, but it also looks at the people within the congregation and in large mass using their numbers to be able to affect change. And that's really not something I had seen or experienced in my clergy profession.

Oftentimes, I would engage in efforts [via] clergy organizations, ministerial organizations, which certainly have their value, but I thought, with respect to mobilizing people for large-scale change, that the community-organizing model, which looks at congregational involvement—at the level of the pastor but also at the level of . . . involving the laity, you know—to me, [that] is a game changer.

I'm focused on . . . a couple different areas: jobs, education, criminal justice, food sustainability, and health care. And so what we do is we get in groups within our respective congregations and research these areas to get a look at some of the best practices . . . and some of the workings in other cities. And we also look at how other community organizations, whether they are religious[ly] based or not, have been able to implement change in their respective regions. . . .

And so we're about forty congregations, and all forty congregations have worked on the issues. . . . We have found that using a community-organizing model that is both regional, not simply urban but regional and suburban, that is diverse religiously—we have Christian congregations, Catholic congregations, synagogues, Islamic mosques—as well as racial diversity. We have found that there has been a great amount of power and influence when we work in coalition. And it's actually been quite successful, I think more successful had we only been focused only at top-tier leadership and not trying to actually mobilize our congregation as a whole.

INTERVIEWER: Can you talk to me a little bit more about what ministerial alliances have done and where you think they could learn, at least, from the model that you're employing with the FBCO?

MILLS: Well, I think, obviously, when one begins to think about organizations, institutions, churches, one thinks about the leader, the pastor, the CEO, the mayor, the president, and what have you. And this can be both nonprofit and full-profit sectors, the faith-based, the community-based sectors, or what have you. . . . I mean, obviously, leaders provide vision and direction to an organization, and they have the ability to influence . . . how the organization moves based on its mission.

At the same time, however, we looked at faith-based organizations, [which] are driven and mobilized around the volunteer base, particularly churches. And so, when we think about the civil rights movement and reflect upon it, what do we think about? We think about the mass meetings. We think about leading the church to go down to downtown Birmingham to protest. Or we think about Dr. King and others encouraging people to stay with the fight. We think about the Montgomery Improvement Association, which was a coalition of clergy leaders, but they were mobilizing people. And so I think that, certainly, there is always going to be value, certainly, to have voices. But there's also something to be said about being able to rally people around taking up their civic responsibility and their social responsibility. . . .

You know, some churches I think they view their pastor as a civil rights leader or a social justice advocate in their respective communities. But . . . when Moses, when they found out that others were prophesying in the camp, they got upset because Moses was the one prophet. There's a line where Moses says, "I would hope that there would be more that would prophesy." You know, or the New Testament passage that says, "In the last days, I will pour out My Spirit on all, that your, our sons and daughters will prophesy." And so, when you begin to see social justice as not just the mission of the minister but the mission of the ministry itself, i.e., the church, it only seems natural. It would only seem the natural by-product that one's whole congregation would be engaged in that work, keeping that historical work going. I think the best of that would be the civil rights movement.

INTERVIEWER: What do you do through the black ministerial alliance?
MILLS: Well, one of the great things with the alliance is it provides a
great clearinghouse for information. With the group meet[ing] on a
weekly basis, we are made aware of new developments. . . . Community leaders, political leaders, public officials will come to those meetings and inform us about what they're doing. So we will be informed
as religious leaders, one, to weigh in on it, to provide feedback.
Sometimes, we'll share this information with our congregation as a
community resource, to communicate information to them. There
are also times when it is necessary that we as Christian leaders speak
out, particularly those who are African American within the city, and
because of the acute issues that affect us here. . . .

  And so the alliance does have certain great value. I can think of
occasions where the alliance's voice has been critical on the issues of
today. . . . The alliance was a part of making awareness of the [school]
issue, supporting the passion for our children. They were a part of
that effort. And so, you know, there's certainly a value to us as ministers coming together, one, as a clearinghouse, as a reader's resource,
as a united voice. But I don't think it's either/or. I think it's mostly a
both/and. And the FBCO, there are a number of African American
ministers who are members of the black ministerial alliance and,
obviously, vice versa.
INTERVIEWER: If you were to choose the top three issues facing the
African American community today, what would those be?
MILLS: Well, I would say, education, criminal justice, and poverty. I
think, obviously, education, . . . particularly urban education, . . . creating equality in the urban education experience or a quality education experience for those in the urban core is critical. You know,
African Americans still continue to live—in large numbers—in
urban settings. And so attacking the problem of urban education
and the inability to produce the kind of quality educational experience . . . that we see in the suburban counterparts, . . . it's a civil rights
issue, since May 17, 1954, *Brown v. Board of Education.* So education
is a civil rights issue. Obviously, the dynamics and the dimensions of
it have changed, but it's still a civil rights issue.

  Poverty, it remains a crucial issue. Again, in [our city], 40 percent
of the residents remain in poverty. And I think that's directly con-

nected to education. I think it's also connected, obviously, to . . . the breakdown of kind of the industrial working centers. And as a result of that, in a . . . professional and technology based industry, African Americans have a great opportunity or the opportunity and job opportunity to raise the quality of life.

But, obviously, the criminal justice system—I mean, it's just education, poverty, and criminal justice are really a triangle. You know, we know what a felony conviction can mean, you know, for a person coming out of prison . . . with a felony conviction: cannot get a student loan, federal student loan, can't get in public housing. You can't get access to social welfare programs. So, once again, . . . the cycle of poverty continues. Obviously, people who . . . have some of these convictions, more than likely, are not going to be able to find a job. So not only are you unskilled, but you have kind of a scarlet letter, you know, of a felony conviction, which kind of debilitates you even further. And, once again, the cycle of poverty . . . continues. So I would say education, poverty, and then criminal justice.

INTERVIEWER: Do you think there's any kind of organized movement in Ohio or nationally addressing any of these issues?

MILLS: What we are seeing in Ohio now is the conversation. I think what you're now seeing is conversation. You know, obviously, the beliefs of Michelle Alexander's book *The New Jim Crow* has really kind of shot off the bow, you know, to kind of raise our awareness, both in the faith community and the traditional civil rights community, you know, to a national audience in general, you know, about—identifies this caste system of those who are victims of the prison industrial complex. What we are seeing is things like the Ohio Collaborative, Ohio Prophetic Voices, which have now started having conversations at a state-wide level around, particularly around the issue of criminal justice, voter empowerment, the securing or the continued protection of voting rights. So I do see early signs of efforts.

Now, the extent to which that actualizes in a mobilized movement remains to be seen. However, you know, the people who I know that are involved in some of these conversations and some of these efforts, you know, are truly people that, you know, are already doing it within their respective communities. It's really a matter of, you know, changing a network into some much more sustained action at a state-wide level.

Peter Mills has chosen a different path of social engagement than Brashear and McCormick, at least at this stage in his career. He was committed to mobilizing for social change through the FBCO model and content with working outside the black church. This does not mean that the black church did not matter to Mills. It did. The black ministerial alliance he was affiliated with was especially helpful as an information repository, a place where black pastors could learn about and share important, relevant information. They developed and refined their collective voice in the alliance. They were also connected with civic leaders. But for Mills, the black ministerial alliance was not the place through which you mobilize for social change. In fact, Mills proposed that it was the FBCO that was carrying on the tradition of mass mobilization honed by Dr. Martin Luther King Jr. and other black religious leaders of the civil rights movement.

Mills also assumed more of an intellectual orientation toward social issues rather than an experiential one. He thought and talked about social inequities as if he were an outsider (e.g., "[It] identifies this caste system of *those* who are victims"), and perhaps he is. He is African American and pastors a congregation of people who are directly affected by the social issues he discussed. But he also has a PhD and graduated from an elite HBCU, experiences not common among African Americans, especially "those" who fall victim to the criminal justice system.

Additionally, rather than rely on personal stories like Brashear and McCormick, Mills riddled off statistics about poverty and unemployment when explaining the social issues he saw as critical. He used academic terminology like the "industrial working centers," "cycles of poverty," and "prison industrial complex." He mentioned that he is very familiar with the *New York Times* best-selling book *The New Jim Crow*. Apparently, Mills had done a good deal of reading and learned many facts about racial inequality in the process. It is quite plausible that Mills's academic orientation to social change was simply an artifact of his limited experience as a head pastor at that time. He had not yet built up a repertoire of personal stories from which to ground his approach to social action, so he relied on broader stories.

Mills's way of engaging social issues through the FBCO and the way he talked about social issues also suggest that he did not see himself as a "black preacher," at least in the traditional sense. Despite having ties to high-status black religious leaders and linking his story to the legacy of the black church, referencing Dr. Martin Luther King Jr. on multiple occasions, he did not feel bound to any expectations that he should invest in the black religious leader community. This could have been potentially problematic. Mark Thompson, whom you met in previous chapters, expressed concerns about Mills's and other young black pastors' approaches to social action. He discussed this topic at length, bringing it up on his own. Here is what he said:

> I think, in some instances, some of the pastors come from . . . Eastern Ivy League seminaries, and I think their training, . . . it's like anti-the-folk church. This is how I interpret it. And I don't ever want to become so educated or so intelligent that I cannot relate to what I call "my everyday-folk pastors." . . . Some of these pastors are very linked to a strong interfaith movement, [an FBCO in the city]. . . . I don't have a problem with that. . . . But I decided that this was a season where a lot of the younger pastors that had come back into [the city] ought to be spending as much time with the black pastors and organizing within the context of the heart and the soul of the black community—versus some larger external interfaith effort.

Clearly, Thompson perceived that young black pastors like Mills ought to be working with their peers who are embedded in the black church rather than working with a diverse organization that is not rooted in the "heart and the soul of the black community." Time will tell if Mills remains invested in the FBCO approach. He was, as of recently, still engaged in FBCO. Several respondents from older generations who also worked with an FBCO at the beginning of their careers did not continue with the FBCO approach. They eventually stopped investing their energies in the FBCO and turned them toward the black religious leader community.

But this is a new generation. Diversity is a dominant value in the United States today, one that is expressed across institutions. If the black religious leader network is not effectively mobilizing for social change that improves the lives of African Americans, then perhaps some of the younger generation of black religious leaders in the twenty-first century will decide that the FBCO approach is the way to go.

* * *

The General, Wyoming Brashear; the Warrior, Brian McCormick; and the Protégé, Peter Mills, mattered because of their high status and leadership on social-justice-related issues within the Ohio black religious network. In many ways, Brashear, McCormick, and Mills are similar. They each have a national presence. They are affiliated with a congregational black denomination. Particularly relevant to the discussion here is their strong sense of connection to and responsibility for the legacy of the civil rights movement and their firm commitment to social justice. Collectively, their stories offer a glimpse into where the black church has been, where it has attempted to go, and where it may be headed in the future, especially when it comes to social and political matters.

Wyoming Brashear embodies the prototypical black religious leader and where the black church has been. He was involved in the civil rights movement, one of the most pivotal historical moments for the black church, African Americans, and Americans generally. He is among a select number of people who can claim to have participated in the civil rights movement, let alone to have been an organizer of local protest events. This biographical fact continued to elevate Brashear's status in the Ohio black religious network. Moreover, his sociopolitical legacy apparently extended beyond Ohio. He served as an adviser for Jesse Jackson and Barack Obama during their runs for the presidency. He remained a sought-after figure, receiving speaking invitations at religious and civic events across the country. And other high-status black religious leaders in this study spoke very highly of Brashear, often with a sense of reverence.

Brashear's ideology, theology, and worldview were informed by his strong identification with the African American story. He integrated the legacy of key African American freedom and religious leaders into his vision of the black church and African American community today. Yet, despite his extensive career and status in the black church, an institution that on a variety of social matters swings right, he continued to evolve in his ideology, theology, and engagement on social justice issues, coming to affirm, over time, more liberal views, particularly on gender and sexuality. In this way, Brashear may not simply symbolize where the black church and its leaders have been but may be continuing to lead the black church into the future.

Brian McCormick stands between the civil rights movement generation of black religious leaders and today's up-and-coming generation. McCormick was mentored by well-known, central figures in the civil rights movement. He respected that generation, the sacrifices they made, and gleaned knowledge from their words and experiences. He assumed the banner they entrusted to him. When the moment chose him (recall that people in the community sought after him when a racial crisis arose), McCormick drew on what he had learned, tapped into the power of the legacy of the civil rights movement black religious leader, and led a local, coordinated "moment" that challenged the modern-day racial hierarchy.

The lesson of McCormick's story, in part, is that the civil rights movement worked. It changed how people in the United States talk about race and how they relate. It impacted institutions, culminating in the elimination of explicitly racist laws and policies. Still, the system—that interconnected, institutionally based set of values, beliefs, and practices—managed to reproduce a racial hierarchy in which blacks remain vulnerable and subordinated. This is what McCormick and the people he led were up against: a less visible yet effective system that threatened their safety, economic security, and life chances.

Two affronts that McCormick and his organization addressed were the murders of unarmed black men by the police and the subsequent justification of these murders and discriminatory service practices of local businesses, practices that appeared to target blacks. They attempted to challenge the evolved white hegemonic system with the tools used to disrupt Jim Crow. He and his activist partners boycotted, marched, made demands of, and negotiated with top government officials. Changes were made, but the extent to which they disrupted the status quo—that is debatable.

Moreover, McCormick's experience heading this struggle was personally depleting. The risk-reward ratio in the end was far from balanced. Who would want to assume this role in the face of such sacrifice and against such an elusive target?

Perhaps this is why Peter Mills has, so far, taken another approach. He primarily cultivated and maintained relationships with two leader networks that had limited overlap and that relied on different social and cultural tools for social action—the black religious leader network and a religiously ecumenical and racially diverse religious network. As he explained, the black religious leader network provided important information about social and political matters in the community as well as access to government and civic leaders. The FBCO allowed him the ability to work with other religious leaders and engage in social action around local social justice issues.

Being embedded in both of these distinct and separate networks was advantageous for Mills from a strictly network structure perspective. He could potentially act as a broker between these networks, negotiating the transmission of resources across these bodies of leaders.[1] However, Mills seemed rather to use his network location to accumulate knowledge and resources for his endeavors and those of his church and others who follow him. He did not discuss acting as a conduit for information and resources across these networks. Perhaps this is because he was unaware of the respect and expectations that some from the older generation of black religious leaders, including Wyoming Brashear, had for him. He was not using his potential influence and capacity to build bridges across these networks because he did not know that he could.

The role that the black religious leader will play in the social and political spheres of the twenty-first century is still in negotiation and remains to be seen. Of course, there will be considerable variation in how people meet the expectations of this role. There always has been. Still, there are some clues in the stories of Brashear, McCormick, and Mills about what will remain consistent. Black religious leaders will continue to be engaged in social and political matters. We see this sustained across generations with Brashear, McCormick, and Mills. Each placed a very high value on social and political engagement. This value was evident in their actions, albeit in different ways. Also, the civil rights movement model of the black religious leader will be the standard against which the black religious leader measures success. The immense respect for what the leaders of the movement achieved has not waned. Mills was born after the assassination of King. Yet the legacy of the civil rights movement and its leaders deeply resonated with him and how he saw himself as a black religious leader.

The experience of Mills suggests, though, that there just might be a sea change in how the younger generation of black religious leaders carries on the torch in this century. If Mills and other younger black religious leaders who are similarly situated in civic and religious leader organizations learn to successfully broker these two kinds of social networks, it could reveal a new path by which black religious leaders can reach across racial lines to mobilize for social change.[2] However, there is a real challenge with this strategy. It may require black religious leaders to share the resources of the black church with FBCOs, not the reverse, as racially diverse religious communities are inclined to follow a white hegemonic cultural model (Edwards 2008; Edwards, Christerson, and Emerson 2013). Thus, there is no incentive for young black religious leaders like Mills to relinquish power over the only black-controlled institution in the United States. However, if FBCOs recognize the institutional capacity of the black church and are willing to share their resources with and follow the lead of black religious leaders and the black church, the way forward for black religious leader mobilization in the twenty-first century might be one that actualizes core values of what the United States has claimed about itself since its inception: justice and equality. Time will tell if such promise will be realized.

Conclusion

Hundreds of people converged on city hall for the Demonstration of Black Excellence. The mayor of the city and several police officers attended the protest as well, which from news coverage we saw was unusual for this city. The crowd was diverse, but most of the people were black men and boys in suits, dress shirts, slacks, and ties. They carried signs with statements like "Not Just an Athlete," "We Are Enough," "Black Excellence," and "Faith over Fear" as they marched around the block. The marchers ended their walk at the steps of the city hall. Upon their arrival, a brief program got under way. Several pastors prayed and shared words with the crowd. As was promised by the local pastor who organized the protest, these pastors too wanted it known that black men were respectable. They deserved dignity and respect. They wanted change. They made their case in their Sunday best. One told the crowd, "We know oftentimes in our community and everywhere, black men are labeled as thugs, violent and aggressive. We know that is not true." Another said, "I would like to see legislation passed to hold officers accountable. If they are not upholding the law, they should be punished. I also want to see more programs where young African Americans can learn about law enforcement." Harking back to the songs of the civil rights movement, the crowd was led to sing "We Shall Overcome" (Starkey 2020).

In this book, we have aimed to address two guiding questions: (1) Do contemporary black religious leaders have the capacity to mobilize in the twenty-first century beyond the local level? (2) If so, how, when, and why do they do so? The preceding chapters have addressed these questions from different angles, using the case of Ohio black religious leaders' mobilization of the black vote in 2012, a moment when the voting rights of blacks were being systematically challenged across the country, including in Ohio, and the first black president was up for reelection. This case allowed us to observe, in real time, contemporary black religious leaders' participation in mobilization that extended beyond the local level.

It should come as no surprise that the people in our study overwhelmingly supported President Barack Obama.[1] Not only were his politics largely aligned with theirs (save his position on same-sex marriage), but in many ways, they identified with him as an educated black male leader in the United States. As they saw it, his fate was their fate. Their standpoint also meant that they were not quick to jump on the postracial bandwagon that was circling around during that time. Closely paying attention to the country's response to President Obama, coupled with their personal experiences as educated black male leaders and knowledge of white evangelicals, they knew better. The United States was by no means postracial, despite having elected a black man as president of the country.

Contrary to what was expected, it was not black religious leaders' overwhelming support for Obama that motivated them to mobilize the black vote during his bid for reelection. They wanted him to be reelected, for sure, but this was not what moved them to try to get others to vote. Two other factors were critical for getting black religious leaders to collectively mobilize. The first was that black pastors in the black religious leader community whom we call principal leaders said they should, and so they did. And the second is that blacks' access to the vote in the state was being threatened. These two factors together motivated a statewide get-out-the-vote effort; and they have something rather important in common. Both are connected to the civil rights movement. Being personally linked, directly or indirectly, to the civil rights movement proved to be a highly valued credential in the black religious leader network, and it, almost singularly, made those who possessed this link eligible to be principal leaders in the black religious community. Principal leaders, supported by high-status leaders in the network, made sense of why black religious leaders and congregants should mobilize by linking their efforts to those of the civil rights movement. The Ohio get-out-the-vote efforts were framed by black religious leaders as a stand against those who would block blacks' access to the vote, a key achievement of the civil rights movement and its pastor leaders.

Under this condition, fighting for voting rights, principal leaders had significant influence. However, we have argued that their power was limited, in part, because of what we call the black Protestant ethic. The black Protestant ethic is a perspective that acknowledges systemic and persistent black structural disadvantage but places responsibility for fixing this structural disadvantage on blacks. Black religious leaders in our study across the board believed in the persistence of racism and discrimination and that these were to blame for black disadvantage. However, a large proportion of them also strongly supported tenets of the Protestant ethic. And when it came to providing solutions to black disadvantage, these leaders tended to default to ones that placed the blame on blacks. From these leaders' perspectives, the problem was that black people did not have a strong work ethic or strong cultural values or keep their heads low, so to speak, by, for example, not hanging out on street corners and giving the impression to authorities that they were up to no good. Consequently, solutions that these black religious leaders gave for the social disadvantages some blacks experience had more to do with how individuals should get it together rather than problems endemic to a racist social system.

Given the historical importance of partnerships with civic organizations like the NAACP and the SCLC, we also talked with black religious leaders about their relationships with these organizations, including their connection with faith-based community organizing, which has increased rather dramatically over recent decades. We learned that, in their view, organizations like the NAACP and the SCLC did not have the organizing capacity that they did decades ago. While a large majority of black religious leaders in our study had memberships in these organizations, they were largely symbolic. When it came to taking action, many in our study instead partnered with local FBCOs. However, these partnerships put them in an interesting and potentially compromising space. On the one hand, FBCOs had the organizing capacity that contemporary black-centered civic organizations seemed to lack. But, on the other hand, the FBCO was an often white-led multiracial, religiously ecumenical coalition. The issues that FBCOs mobilized for were general to the coalition and many times prioritized white liberal aims. Even when FBCOs did include black issues in their agenda, it was rare for these multi-issue organizations to put their full weight behind any one campaign for an extended period of time. When they did, it was usually for an issue that included the whole multiracial base (e.g., health care, housing, education) rather than issues that were "particular" to one constituency (e.g., racism in policing). This was the case in 2012, when we collected our data.

Consequently, black religious leaders who partnered with FBCOs could find themselves using their resources and those of their churches for social change campaigns designed and led by white liberals. While these campaigns were aimed at improving the lives of many people, including black people, fighting racism was not the main focus. There was often very little that was particularly black about these campaigns with regard to their rhetoric, leadership, or mobilization tactics. This can be challenging for black religious leaders involved with FBCOs because the issues they were encouraged to focus on were not necessarily the ones that galvanize black communities the most. One consequence of this dynamic is that black religious leaders could not gain the same kind of prestige in their own communities through participating in FBCO campaigns that they could receive through participating in social action organic to black religious leader communities.

Finally, in chapter 6, we focused on three people in our sample who represented three generations of black religious leaders. They all had been actively involved in social justice issues, mobilizing people in their communities as well as other black religious leaders. Their unique stories highlight how generational differences and the broader social context can affect how black religious leaders think about and engage social action.

Black Ministers and Mobilization in the Twenty-First Century

In response to our first question, whether contemporary black religious leaders have the capacity to mobilize beyond the local level in the twenty-first century, the answer is yes. Contemporary black religious leaders can effectively mobilize for social issues beyond the local level. What we observed were loosely connected yet highly coordinated efforts by black religious leaders aimed at mobilizing the black vote across the state. Their efforts seem to have paid off. Black voters came out in record numbers that year. This suggests that black religious leaders' capacity for mobilization beyond the local level remains strong and effective.

Once it was established that black religious leaders most likely have the capacity to mobilize beyond the local level, our follow-up questions, then, were when, how, and why they do so. We proposed that the civil rights movement legacy, in a very real sense, determines the answers to those questions. This legacy remains quite powerful after more than fifty years and is perhaps the most central organizing cultural characteristic of the contemporary black religious leader community. Contemporary black religious leaders in our study continued to see their counterparts who led in the civil rights movement as representing the quintessential black pastor and the ones they desired to emulate. The civil rights movement legacy also influenced the kinds of issues they mobilized for (or not), how they justified their engagement in social action, the reasons they gave to motivate others to get involved, and who got to lead their mobilization efforts. This influence had critical implications for their mobilizing capacity.

Nevertheless, despite the capacity to mobilize at least at the state level, contemporary black religious leaders in our study were not involved in or aware of any recent broad-based efforts among their peers that targeted undoing systemic racism, particularly that which disadvantages blacks. This was surprising to us. During these interviews, we were already in a moment in history when national mobilization against systems legitimating deadly gun violence against unarmed black men was under way. If there was any time for contemporary black religious leaders to hit the streets, it seemed that this was as good a time as any.

Looking from the outside in, it may make little sense that contemporary black religious leaders have not been central to the Black Lives Matter movement or other similar movements aimed at redressing black oppression, given the role they have played as leaders and advocates for justice and equality for black communities. Not only is there a precedent that they would lead, but collectively they have considerable power and influence over essential resources for effective mobilization, like space and professional staff, not to mention material resources such as vehicles, computers, audiovisual equipment, office supplies, and so on. Simply having the ear of people who respect you and take seriously what you say is a vitally important resource as well.

We have argued that there are good reasons why contemporary black religious leaders may not collectively leverage these resources to launch and lead broad-based mobilization efforts challenging contemporary racial injustice. They have to do with factors that are both internal and external to the black religious leader community. These factors together create structures that guide sometimes, constrain at other times, and can even leave black religious leaders virtually powerless as leaders of social action under certain conditions.[2]

Challenges Within and Without

People do life in groups. Groups are critically important to how people make their way in the world and how they see and understand themselves. People are members of a host of groups: religious groups, age-related groups, gender groups, clubs, social organizations, work-related groups. The list goes on. However, in the United States, one's racial and ethnic groups are powerfully important. This has to do with the value the country places on racial and ethnic identity. We can point to race-based laws diminishing or denying people's humanity, their right to freedom, and even their right to life on the basis of their race or the forced segregation and genocide of people who were not labeled as white. Then there is the history of eugenics, which ranked people's supposed genetic value on the basis of their country or region of origin, so that certain racial and ethnic groups were considered less desirable humans than other racial and ethnic groups were. Laws, policies, and ideologies such as these organize people and distribute valuable resources, like freedom and wealth, along racial and ethnic lines. The outcome is very sharp boundaries drawn around racial and ethnic groups.

After racial and ethnic boundaries are delineated, in large part because of outside pressures, people go about making meaning of their groups. Groups use "culture and history to create common meanings, to build solidarity, and to launch social movements" (Nagel 1994, 161). Joane Nagel (1994) uses the image of a shopping cart to illustrate how groups select particular "goods," that is, various cultural elements and historical narratives, to fill the cart and then use these goods to tell themselves and others who they are and what they are about. We can think of the civil rights movement legacy as a good in the shopping cart of contemporary black religious leaders that they use to define the group. Like a ready-made meal, this legacy contains built-in, highly valuable, understood cultural symbols like music, speaking style, stories, beliefs, dress, narratives, and physical spaces (e.g., churches), among others that they can readily draw on to aid in maintaining solidarity and providing direction for the group. The value that the United States on the whole places on the civil rights movement and Dr. Martin Luther King Jr. gives these cultural symbols remarkable staying power and purchase not only in the black religious leader community but outside it as well. The civil rights movement legacy thus anchors the black religious leader community in powerful ways.

Additionally, the civil rights movement legacy provides a blueprint for how black religious leaders can successfully effect change. What black religious leaders achieved with the civil rights movement some might say was miraculous. Here was a marginalized group that had been viciously oppressed for hundreds of years that organized a mass movement challenging their oppressors, a movement that extended across multiple states and placed such pressure on local, state, and national governments that they bent to its will, by either reacting to its tactics as they wanted (e.g., jailing people, violence, etc.) or changing the law. The movement took patience, courage, strategy, organizational structure, discipline, and vision. The civil rights movement was so successful that it made scholars pay attention and rethink how they theorize about and study social movements (e.g., McCarthy and Zald 1977; McAdam 1986, 88; Morris 1981, 1984).

Yet, despite the many reasons that the civil rights movement legacy is so important for contemporary black religious leaders, it at the same time renders the mobilization capacity of black religious leaders inflexible. It dictates in many ways when, how, and why they mobilize. This dynamic is expected given that black religious leaders are a group with a high level of solidarity and deep sense of who they are and desire to be. The group has clear cultural symbols that communicate its boundaries. Groups with firm boundaries and cultural symbols have established and agreed-on understandings of what "getting things done" looks like. While disagreements and conflicts will arise, established cultural symbols help bring people back to the table. Indeed, all groups, if they are to have a high level of solidarity and a clear sense of identity and direction, need to have firm boundaries and understood, agreed-on cultural symbols. Groups that do not have shared boundaries and cultural symbols typically experience low levels of solidarity and an ambiguous sense of identity. As you can imagine, this is not helpful for getting things done.

Still, if the shopping cart only has ingredients for a fish fry and tomorrow's the annual family BBQ, something in the cart has got to change if a proper BBQ is going to take place. And that is the challenge. The shopping cart of contemporary black religious leaders has the ingredients for a delectable fish fry, but it lacks the necessary ingredients for a wonderful BBQ. Or as Ann Swidler (1986) puts it, their cultural toolkit, which is so heavily dependent on the civil rights movement legacy, has the tools at the ready to address any issue that aligns well with the aims and strategies of the movement and probably quite successfully. But their cultural toolkit lacks the proper tools for addressing an issue that does not align well with civil rights movement aims and strategies.

Why might this be? We have to remember that the racism of the Jim Crow era, especially in the South, was the in-your-face kind of racism. There was no misunderstanding. There was no backpedaling or trying to hide what was really meant. People owned their belief in the superiority of whites and whiteness. Similarly, the racial injustice was reinforced by explicitly racial local and state laws. Whites belong over here, going through the front door, where all the desirable goods of society are. These include certain entertainment establishments and restaurants, better neighborhoods, school resources, better jobs, more seating on public transportation, and so on. Blacks belong over there, meant for backdoor service and access, if any at all.

The cultural tools of the civil rights movement initially targeted the Jim Crow South. They were created or selected to address this kind of racial system, one that was explicit, named, and clear. Before the assassination of Dr. Martin Luther King Jr., the SCLC made attempts to apply these tools to issues that were nationally relevant, like unfair housing and the Vietnam War. However, the civil rights movement legacy has not included these streams of the movement in the broader narrative. The tools that have been esteemed and sharpened are those that were used to challenge the Jim Crow South. However, contemporary US racism looks different from that of the Jim Crow South. While scholars of post-civil-rights-era racism may not agree on what to call it or how to precisely measure it, they do agree on one thing; today's racism is for the most part indirect, implicit, and unspoken. It is a system in which you know you keep getting slapped but you are not sure when those hits are coming or where exactly they are coming from.

In many ways, contemporary racism looks like the racism of the North during the Jim Crow era and even well before that. W. E. B. Du-Bois, for example, describes in *The Souls of Black Folk* ([1903] 2008) the subtle way that supposedly more enlightened whites of the time questioned blacks about what it was like to be a "problem." He talks about the painful, quiet racism he felt as a child in Massachusetts. He tells of the racism that Alexander Crummell experienced as a black minister in a white denomination. Similarly, today, dog-whistle politics and hidden racist messages remain par for the course, even in a moment when explicit racism by some people can continue on without consequence. People who claim to be well-meaning reinforce a white-supremacist social system by reinforcing white hegemony (Edwards 2008; Hughey 2012; Bell and Hartmann 2007). People work rather hard to appear not to be racist (Gallagher 2003; Bonilla-Silva and Forman 2000). Covert forms of racism and racial discrimination are the ones that are trickiest and most difficult to oppose. It is these forms of racism and racial discrimination that have been the stealthiest, most recalcitrant, and most persistent. The civil rights movement cultural toolkit was not made to combat this sort of racialized system.

The other internal factor is the black Protestant ethic. Recall that the pastors in our study who held to a black Protestant ethic believed that racism in the United States was a major factor when it came to blacks' systemic disadvantage. But when it came to concrete explanations, the pastors would pivot to individualistic solutions that consistently placed the blame on those who were disadvantaged. Not everyone in our study held to the black Protestant ethic. It is, therefore, not nearly as core to the cultural toolkit as the civil rights movement legacy is. Still, a slight majority of the black religious leaders we spoke with affirmed it. That would be more than enough to create a real challenge to mass mobilization among black religious leaders that targets systemic racism and discrimination.

Interestingly, the high degree of solidarity that the civil rights movement legacy provides black religious leaders may actually work against mobilization as well. High solidarity is a real asset for mobilization. Division can splinter a movement, leaving it ineffective as resources are split up. However, when a large proportion of a group does not really believe in the aims of a potential movement yet are at the same time understood to be legitimate group members, this complicates building consensus around an issue. You cannot simply push legitimate members of the group aside. Group membership means they matter, as do their views and perspectives. The black Protestant ethic has to be accounted for when considering issues for which to mobilize.

The civil rights movement legacy and the black Protestant ethic are factors internal to the black religious leader community that affect its mobilization capacity. But it is not just factors internal to the black religious community that matter. The contemporary racial system and changes in the social organization field are structural factors external to the community that impact black religious leaders' mobilization as well.

The contemporary racial system in the United States originates with the end of the civil rights movement. The monumental legislative reforms that came in the wake of the movement's pressure changed the country. The Civil Rights Act of 1964, the Immigration and Nationality Act of 1965, the Voting Rights Act of 1965, and the Fair Housing Act of 1968 impacted how people do life, whom they work with, live near, see on the streets, go to school with, and sit near in public spaces and how they are represented in government, among a myriad of other changes. Yet, despite these changes, the laws did not undo race in the United States. Race arguably remains the most central organizing feature of the US landscape (Omi and Winant 1994). There is no time in US history when race was not critical to the structuring of everyday life, save perhaps for a very brief period during the early years of colonization. The post-civil-rights United States is no different. The country has shown itself to be quite good at reinventing new ways of maintaining a white-supremacist society after taking major blows to the status quo. Just as DuBois in *The Souls of Black Folk* ([1903] 2008) laments how the ending of slavery did not mean true freedom and opportunity for blacks, noting the pervasiveness and persistence of white supremacy in the North and the South, scholars of the post-civil-rights era show that legislation of the 1960s did not mean true freedom and opportunity for blacks and other people of color, again noting the pervasiveness and persistence of white supremacy.

The reproduction of white dominance can be attributed to a process of racial formation. Racial formation is "the sociohistorical process by which racial categories are created, inhabited, transformed, and destroyed" (Omi and Winant 1994, 55). It is the outcome of racial projects that include "an effort to reorganize and redistribute resources along particular racial lines" (56). Racial formation is in effect a hegemonic process, one based on race. The reason why the United States is able to maintain a social system that privileges whites is because it is so good at being a hegemony. Hegemonies are power systems based on the acquiescence of subordinate groups to the status quo. This acquiescence can look like endorsement or resignation or somewhere in between.

Successful hegemonies are ones that make everyday life seem normal, just the way things are and ought to be, not only for the dominant group but for subordinate groups as well. This means that they control what is understood to be dominant culture, that is, societal values, beliefs, ideologies, thought paradigms, customs, folkways, and mores, as well as the kinds of material culture like food, dress, hairstyles, music, and technology. Just as culture is used to delineate who is legitimate and who is not for black religious leaders, dominant culture signifies who best represents what it means to be a member of a society, who is a legitimate member, and who is not. The thing about hegemonies is that they are structured to privilege the already powerful. Really successful hegemonies, however, are adept at seeming to be for everyone, both the already powerful and the less powerful.

Let us look at an example. The dominant ideology of the United States asserts that freedom and opportunity are available for everyone. Liberty is a human right, a God-ordained one, according to the sacred documents of the United States. We have heard it before: "We hold these truths to be self-evident, that all men are created equal, that they are endowed by their Creator with certain unalienable Rights, that among these are Life, Liberty and the pursuit of Happiness." Yet this has not stopped the United States from finding ways to justify systemic racial hierarchies and to codify these justifications in laws and policies. In the past, racism and discrimination have been explicit. Today, they are implicit.

Now, one of the challenges with effective social movements is that they need a frame that both is flexible and can handle refutation (Benford and Snow 2000) as well as that can be "congruent both with the cultural framework of the challenging community and their main organizational vehicles" (Morris 2000, 449). The brilliance of the civil rights movement mobilization frame is that it was able to do this well. By, in part, developing a frame that drew on the sacred ideologies of the United States, it exposed the hypocrisy of the country, in a moment when the United States wanted to be seen globally as a beacon of freedom and democracy. Yet this frame had a downfall. By holding the country accountable to its own rhetoric, the movement affirmed the United States (Omi and Winant 1994). It was not that the very foundations of the country were corrupt. Rather, it just had not lived up to its own ideals. In this, the framing of the movement did not take aim at the hegemonic structure. It only took aim at what could be construed as terribly unfortunate outcomes of an otherwise good system.

And in response, the United States did what hegemonies do best. It incorporated parts of the civil rights movement frame, that people were no longer to be judged by the "color of their skin," and repurposed the meaning of the frame. The famous adage not to judge people by the color of their skin was intended to inspire change that ensured equal social and economic outcomes by race. What emerged was a new kind of racism that was "kinder and gentler" (Bobo, Kluegel, and Smith 1996) and hid behind a claim of colorblindness (Bonilla-Silva 2001) but was just as effective at maintaining the already established racial hierarchy. Even though race had explicitly been used as a reason to create racial systems that excluded and oppressed people since the land was colonized, this new narrative asserts that racism and racial discrimination are not an acceptable explanation for why groups experience systemic socioeconomic disadvantage and harm. It is rather people's culture, behaviors, and choices that lead to these outcomes.

The Black Lives Matter movement has challenged this racial narrative that has dominated the United States for nearly fifty years. In 2020, the BLM protests worked to move systemic racism back into political discourse. Even the 2020 Democratic convention and the party's then candidates for president and vice president, Joe Biden and Kamala Harris, were talking about systemic racism. And later President-Elect Joe Biden in a speech noted how police forces and the national guard responded to BLM protestors with considerable presence and force, but a violent pro-Trump, largely white mob at the US Capitol was met with little presence or violent reactions. Still, despite recognition of white supremacy, this discourse remains situated within a broader narrative that the United States just has to live up to its ideals.

Alternatively, civil rights movement leaders could have taken direct aim at the white-supremacist superstructure and the ideology that supports it. White supremacy was well established prior to the writing of the country's sacred documents and is what roots US society. Of course, it would have been quite difficult for a frame challenging the white-supremacist superstructure to have ever gotten any traction, given what it takes to construct successful frames. Linking a movement frame in some way to the dominant ideology may have simply been unavoidable, if indeed the aims of the movement were anything short of a full-scale revolution.

This is precisely the same challenge that contemporary black religious leaders face. One critical difference, however, for them is that the frame used by the civil rights movement was co-opted and modified by the dominant group and then absorbed into the hegemonic structure (Omi and Winant 1994). Whites, on average, remained most advantaged in the social system, receiving better jobs with greater pay and power as well as greater wealth and educational opportunities, among a myriad of other benefits, than people of color do. And racism and racial discrimination could no longer be named as the culprit that organizes the whole of the United States along racial lines, whether that be friendship groups, marriages, neighborhoods, churches, occupations, social and recreational organization, schools, or so on. If contemporary black religious leaders are going to successfully harness the resources that they control to impact social change, they will have to mobilize around a frame that challenges today's white-supremacist society, not that of the Jim Crow era.

Some contemporary black religious leaders have opted to collaborate with FBCOs to build effective frames and coalitions in this new racial environment. This brings us to the last factor that we argue impacts the mobilization of contemporary black religious leaders. We propose that an ever-increasing presence of FBCOs in the social movement field over recent decades, combined with a declining role of black-centered movement organizations, has potentially hindered the collective mobilization of contemporary black religious leaders. Given that the main aim of FBCOs is to address social inequality in one form or another, it might seem ironic that they can present challenges to black religious leader mobilization. However, there are two reasons FBCOs can do so. One is that the Saul Alinsky model, which significantly informs the organizing of most FBCOs,[3] and the civil rights movement model, while similar in some ways, are different in other ways that are not easily reconcilable. The second reason is that FBCOs can work to divide and disperse the resources of the black religious leader community.

Before we discuss the differences between the Alinsky model and the civil rights movement model of organizing, let us look at some similarities. One similarity is that both models support organic movements. Alinsky (1941) argues that effective community organizing is best led by the people affected by structures of social disadvantage because they best understand the impact that broader social forces have had on them and what needs to be addressed to rectify them. The civil rights movement was birthed in the black community, led by blacks, and tackled issues germane to blacks. Another similarity is the importance of religious organizations for organic mobilization. Churches and ministers were core to the civil rights movement. Alinsky also recognized that religious organizations are critical for organizing because they are primary spaces that groups use to build community, promote social bonds, and connect people to dominant society. While this is true for any group, it is especially true for those that are socially disadvantaged. Additionally, both the Alinsky model and the civil rights movement model utilize a network of different types of organizations to mobilize. The Alinsky model encourages collaboration across a variety of not-for-profit organizations, including unions, neighborhood councils, and religious organizations from different faiths. The civil rights movement was a collaborative effort of churches as well as other organizations like the Student Nonviolent Coordinating Committee (SNCC), the National Association for the Advancement of Colored People (NAACP), and the Congress of Racial Equality (CORE). Generally speaking, then, the Alinsky model used by FBCOs and that of the civil rights movement overlap a good deal. They both affirm organic movements that are composed of multiple not-for-profit organizations but in which religious organizations are central.

The differences between the models show up in the execution. FBCOs organize local communities and neighborhoods to address a specific, local issue within a specific time frame. Some faith-based community organizing has expanded to regional and statewide efforts; but this is not the norm, and competing national networks can make it difficult for groups to cooperate with one another. The civil rights movement, on the other hand, was a coordinated, multistate movement. The tactics were local, but the agenda was broad. It targeted long-term, systemic racism and discrimination. Moreover, there was no internally imposed time frame on the effort. The organizing continued for decades. In contrast, FBCOs often have commitments to pursue particular issue campaigns based on short-term funding streams from foundations.

Furthermore, FBCOs promote racial and ethnic diversity, but they are still mainly led by white professional staff and are accountable to predominantly white funders (see Oyakawa 2017). The civil rights movement was also diverse. White ministers eventually got involved. CORE was a racially diverse organization. But the civil rights movement was an effort led by African Americans. Faith-based community organizing promotes ecumenism, not just among Christian traditions but among all faith traditions. The civil rights movement was religiously ecumenical too. Catholics, Mainline Protestants, Orthodox Christians, and Jews were involved. Black Methodist Episcopal denominations were involved as well. But, by and large, the religious organizations and leaders were African American Baptists.

FBCOs are thus a largely white-led, diverse, ecumenical, local effort that targets very specific issues within a relatively short span of time. The civil rights movement, on the other hand, was a black-led, somewhat diverse, national effort that aimed to undo systemic racial injustice that oppressed African Americans. And the religious leaders in the movement were mainly African American Baptists. The model used in FBCOs has not accommodated broad, persistent mobilization that challenges systemic issues experienced by a particular ethnoracial group. Yet this is precisely what black religious leaders have historically done, including those who led in the civil rights movement.

Looking at these differences between the organizing models, we see that the Alinsky model used in most FBCOs does not fit well into a cultural toolkit in which the civil rights movement legacy is prominent. A critical implication of black religious leaders aligning with FBCOs is that they will be hindered in their ability to mobilize for social change that is specifically germane to the experiences of blacks. Mary Pattillo-

McCoy (1998) finds black church culture to be an essential component of effective social action in the black community. The freedom of black religious leaders who work with FBCOs to lead in ways that are in line with black church culture may be stifled, if not altogether eliminated. Another is that black religious leaders who participate in faith-based community organizing have to supplant, at least partially, a core cultural characteristic of what it means to be a black religious leader if they are going to engage in FBCO work. They risk compromising their connectedness to the black religious leader community and their own sense of identity as black religious leaders as they invest their time, energy, and other resources elsewhere.

This implication leads us to the other way FBCOs present a challenge to collaborative black religious leader mobilization. They compete for the resources of black religious leaders. People and organizations do not have unlimited resources. As black religious leaders use their resources and those under their influence to advance the aims of an FBCO's agenda, they by definition are diverting resources, at least in part, away from the black religious leader community and any potential aims it may be pursuing. And since FBCOs are taking up more and more space in the social movement field, they could tap into—and tap out—the resources of enough black religious leaders so as to prevent or cripple any collaborative black religious leader effort from even getting off the ground.

To be fair, we cannot know whether black religious leaders would be engaging in such an effort in the absence of FBCOs. It is entirely possible that they would not, given the factors we discussed earlier (i.e., the black Protestant ethic, the mismatch between cultural toolkit of civil rights and contemporary racism, anemic black civic organizations). So perhaps FBCOs are the best possible option right now for pastors who are interested in participating in or leading social movement activities. But regardless of how we frame/understand the dynamic between FBCOs and black religious leader collaboratives, it is true that the existence of FBCOs makes black religious leaders' choices about how to engage in social and political mobilization more complicated and diffuses their resources across a wider range of campaigns and organizations. This impacts the possibility of black religious leaders spearheading a focused movement for black freedom in the United States today.

A Brighter Future

Black Lives Matter is a movement developed and led by black people who do not wear smart suits or have civil rights movement credentials. Yet it is organically black and has become a diverse global movement with people from a variety of races, ethnicities, religions, ages, sexualities, genders, classes, and nationalities. The flexibility and global impact of the hashtag-turned-movement may have been precisely what was needed to challenge white-supremacist patriarchal societies in the twenty-first century. Yet black religious leaders continue to have an unparalleled legacy of effective resistance. They continue to have the capacity to coordinate broad-based mobilization efforts, if our study is any indication, in a way that may also still be needed. But our study suggests that some things have to change if they want to expand their capacity to mobilize in this contemporary context. We propose some thoughts that might be considered.

What we must first remember is that community matters for people. It matters tremendously. And it is shared culture that holds communities together. Everyone is subject to the constraints imposed by the structures and cultures of the communities in which they are embedded. Being a part of a community means that you are responsible to that community. However, at the same time, what constrains us sustains us. We reap benefits for being a part of communities too. Black religious leaders are no different. Their community matters to them. They need to cultivate the structural and cultural material that binds their community. The civil rights movement legacy makes up in no small way the material that sustains the black religious leader community. It is what helps maintain their bonds and sense of connectedness, something that is important not only for social action but for their personal health as well.

Recognizing the value of community and the importance of the civil rights movement legacy for sustaining the community, we propose that increasing black religious leaders' capacity to mobilize requires (1) broadening what motivates mobilization and (2) expanding the boundaries of who is seen as a legitimate contemporary black religious leader, making sure in the process that the civil rights movement legacy remains intact. We suggest that broadening the motivating factor for mobilization minimally means claiming freedom—physical, intellectual, emotional, spiritual, material—as the goal rather than simply gaining rights or protecting those that are being threatened. Rights are a part of freedom, but people can have rights and still not be free. Enslavement can be achieved through a variety of social mechanisms. Recent work on the history and current state of mass incarceration (Alexander 2010; Wacquant 2014) as well as the welfare state (Wacquant 2014), for example, situates this process in our contemporary context. We must not forget, too, that the civil rights movement was at one time the Freedom Movement.[4] Drawing on a narrative of freedom, rather than just rights, is actually a reclamation of the original frame of the movement. The task at hand, then, is to focus on every institution in society, isolate where freedom is systematically restricted for blacks and other people of color in each institution, and target the structures, informal and formal, that limit that freedom. This is, of course, far easier said than done. Our main point is that at a minimum, the frame must expand beyond rights. Using freedom is to continue the original frame for the movement.

The iconic religious leaders of the civil rights movement are educated black men smartly dressed in suit and tie. Decades of repeatedly seeing this image in the media has conditioned us to think that only those black religious leaders who look this way and present themselves in this manner are the ones who can legitimately lead collective social action within the black church, if not the black community. Expanding the boundaries of who can qualify as a principal leader will expand the flexibility of the movement as well as its resources, social and cultural. The two groups we believe ought to be brought to the center of the black religious leader community are young black religious leaders and black women religious leaders. People from these groups have standpoints that traditional black religious leaders do not have. Their standpoints allow them to see and understand the white-supremacist system in different and important ways. Young black religious leaders will have greater access than traditional black religious leaders to other young people whom they can mobilize for social action. They will also have an insight into contemporary racism and racial discrimination that is not filtered through a civil-rights-movement-era lens perhaps like that of their older counterparts. Black women Christians have always been active participants and leaders in the civil rights movement and other acts of resistance and mobilization.[5] Harriet Tubman, Ida B. Wells, Rosa Parks, and Fannie Lou Hamer are iconic examples of black women of faith leading courageously and effectively. Whether that be struggles against slavery, lynching, segregation, mass incarceration, or police killings of unarmed black men or for women's right to vote, black women, often black women of faith, have led in the fight. Their voices have always been there, just suppressed and largely left behind the scenes. It is due time that black women religious leaders be given prominence at the table of power in the black religious leader community, that they are seen and heard and followed.

Black Lives Matter is not the only issue for which black religious leaders can mobilize. There are poverty, human trafficking, and mass incarceration, among many others. BLM is the one that has garnered the most attention and action so far this century. It is difficult to know how long or effective the BLM movement will be. As of the writing of this book, changes have already taken place in response to protests. Local governments are changing policing policies, the US Congress is working on bills to do the same, Confederate flags are being banned, statues symbolizing white supremacy are being taken down, and city streets are being painted with Black Lives Matter across the country. These changes are pushing the struggle for freedom forward.

Black religious leaders, while not at the forefront of the BLM movement, are present. When they are, it is often in a good suit with a nice matching tie. Most people can appreciate a person in a smart suit from time to time. For black religious leaders, men especially, putting on a good suit may even connect them and others to a legacy that they deeply cherish, reminding them of who they are and the mantle they carry. We imagine that it can stir up a sense pride in anyone. Yet it is time to expand the wardrobe, literally and metaphorically, of those who are to lead the freedom struggle to include some jeans, cargo pants, and skirts, as well as dresses, T-shirts, flannel, blouses, and so on. The boots worn by the smartly suited black religious leaders have taken the struggle for freedom a very long way. But these have perhaps become a bit worn down. And there is still a long road ahead in the struggle for freedom. A new pair of boots is in order now as well.

APPENDIX

Methodology

Scholars aim to engage in thoughtful, rigorous research. But no scholar can claim objectivity. We recognize, in line with black feminist epistemology, that our standpoints matter, as do all people's, for the questions we ask and how we come to answer them. The motivation for this book stems from our intellectual interests, for sure, but it is also informed by our personal journeys. So here we share just a bit about ourselves with readers to inform the lens through which we came to this study and wrote this book.

I, Korie Little Edwards, am a scholar of race and religion who is particularly interested in how these two social factors inform each other, mainly in the US context. I am an African American woman. I grew up, save a couple relatively brief stints in Washington, DC, and Ohio, in the city of Pittsburgh, Pennsylvania. I moved to Chicago for college and lived there for a large part of my adult life before moving to Ohio, where I now reside. I am also a Christian. I have been since I was a child. My family church for much of my upbringing took place in a large black Baptist church with a bit of a Pentecostal flair. As an adult, I briefly attended a predominantly white megachurch. But for most of my adult life, I have been a member of either a black church or a multiracial church headed by a black pastor. It is my hope that my scholarship also has practical implications, helping religious organizations and their leaders better understand how race and other societal-level structures impact what they do and why.

My (Michelle Oyakawa's) research agenda emphasizes specifying how organizations can build movements for racial justice. I am half white, half Japanese American (fourth generation in the United States). Both of my parents were born and raised in Ohio, and I grew up in Wadsworth, Ohio. I was an organizer with an FBCO called ISAIAH in Minnesota from 2009 to 2010, and I have conducted several research studies on FBCOs and other social movement organizations over the past decade. While I grew up Christian and was confirmed in the United Methodist Church, I no longer identify as a Christian. My dissertation research was a qualitative study of the Ohio Organizing Collaborative and found that FBCOs and allied organizations face severe limitations because of their reliance on funding from foundations; this has influenced my perspective about these organizations and the movements they create.

The study we use for this book is the Religious Leaders and Civic Activity in Ohio Project. It was partially funded by a grant from the Ruth Landes Foundation. The project takes cues from Morris's *The Origins of the Civil Rights Movement* (1984), which argues that the black church, as an institution, had considerable human, organizational, and material resources that were harnessed to launch and execute a mass protest movement. This "collective power of churches," as he calls it, was essential to the effectiveness of the civil rights movement of the 1950s and 1960s, and it rested on the social networks of black religious leaders. For sure, the members and culture of the black church mattered. There is considerable evidence that these too are vital to the success of African American civic and political engagement (Pattillo-McCoy 1998; Morris 1984; Harris 1994, 1999; Lincoln and Mamiya 1990). But the human, cultural, and financial resources that are embedded in the black church must first be activated and then consolidated by black religious leaders, the gatekeepers to congregations, before they can be deployed for mobilization. We, therefore, focused on black religious leaders in this study, their views and actions, and their relationships to one another and to civic leaders.

The primary aim of the project was to understand black religious leaders' participation in civic and political activity in the state, particularly voter-mobilization efforts during the 2012 election. As noted in the introduction, the case for this study has several theoretically relevant benefits. It was conducted in a historically important moment when the first and only black president was up for reelection, Republican state governments across the country were aiming to change voting opportunities that would negatively affect African Americans, and Black Lives Matter was just gaining steam. It also was a moment when collective broad mobilization by black religious leaders was evident.

The study was conducted in Ohio. In addition to being a key battleground state during the 2012 election, Ohio is the seventh-most-populated state in the country. It is also a diverse state in a lot of ways. It has diverse economies, best represented in its three largest metro areas: Cleveland, Columbus, and Cincinnati. Cleveland, for instance, is a rust-belt city with an economy that is still recovering from deindustrialization. Columbus, on the other hand, has a strong service-based economy and a relatively strong black middle class. It is also headquarters to several large companies, including Nationwide and Victoria's Secret, and is the capital of the state. Cincinnati has a mixed economy as well, with manufacturing, finance, and retail companies headquartered there, including Proctor and Gamble, AK Steel, and Western and Southern Financial. All three cities have large universities, with Columbus having one of the largest in the country, The Ohio State University. Ohio has diverse regional influences too. It is a midwestern state that borders Canada to the north, the eastern United States in Pennsylvania, and the US South with Kentucky along its southwest border. Additionally, there are chapters of all of the major black-centered civic organizations in the state, including the Urban League, the NAACP, the National Action Network, and the SCLC. Thus, black religious leaders have an opportunity to partner with a variety of black-centered civic organizations. Finally, the black religious leader community has historical ties to southern black leaders of the civil-rights-era SCLC. The most notable one is Frederick Shuttlesworth, a key activist in the civil rights movement with the SCLC who is from the South and founded and pastored his church in Cincinnati. Interestingly, neither Shuttlesworth's church nor its pastor emerged as particularly central to the mobilization efforts going on in the state. They were not mentioned by people in our study.

The case included fifty-four in-depth interviews. Forty-three of the interview participants were black religious leaders, including reverends, pastors, and bishops. Eleven of the interview participants were heads of civic organizations who work with or want to work with black religious leaders. These included both black-centered civic organizations and faith-based community organizations. Interviews with black religious leaders are most central to the study. However, civic-related activities in which black religious leaders were actively engaged were observed. And public data (e.g., hardcopy documents, websites, journalistic articles) on the religious and civic organizations of interview participants were compiled. The study's multimethod approach facilitated triangulation of data, providing increased validity and greater insight into the phenomenon studied.

As the intent of this study was, in part, to gain a sense of the extent to which black religious leaders in the state collectively organized for civic and political ends, a sampling strategy was developed that privileged black religious leaders who were well-known, networked, or high status. Several strategies were used toward this end. At the beginning of the sampling process, interview participants were found through multiple avenues: newspaper articles identifying black religious leaders involved in civic and political activity; denominations' and ministerial alliances' lists of affiliated head clergy; and websites on black community resources.

After the data-collection process began, interviews were also used to identify potential participants. Interview participants were asked to name black religious leaders in the state who they perceived to be (1) very active in civic and political activity and/or (2) influential among black religious leaders. Those who were named by three or more interview participants were pursued for interviews.

The sampling strategy yielded a diverse sample. About a fifth of the sample is made up of high-status black religious leaders. A large majority has a college education, and a sizable minority has graduate degrees. Interview participants ranged in age from their early thirties to the early eighties. They headed churches all over the state, particularly in metro areas. And their congregations were affiliated with a variety of Christian traditions, although about two-thirds headed congregations affiliated with black denominations. There is one area that stands out where the sample is not diverse. That is gender. All but two of the interview respondents are men. As we have discussed elsewhere,

> Most black religious leaders in the sample were embedded in formal religious networks, through their affiliation with ministerial alliances or faith-based community. There appeared to be relatively few black head clergypersons in the state of Ohio who led congregations affiliated with nonblack denominations or that are unaffiliated. We invested considerable energy searching for them, calling denomination and association

leaders and asking for recommendations by other pastors, as well as conducting extensive website searches. They may have perhaps been present, but they were not linked to the core of the black religious leader network in the state nor were they easily accessible via other avenues. So, the sample is not representative of black religious leaders. While it might be useful for comparative purposes to have more respondents in the sample who are less connected, for the main focus of this study, an emphasis on embedded and higher-status black religious leaders has at least one important benefit: it is these leaders who would have greater potential to influence the views and actions of other religious leaders, as well as those of their congregants and blacks more broadly. (Edwards 2016, 274–75)

As for interviews with the heads of civic organizations, a list of city- and state-level civic organizations that work with black religious leaders in Ohio was developed. This list includes faith-based community organizing affiliated with organizations like PICO (now Faith in Action) and race-based civic organizations like the Urban League and the NAACP. Twenty organizations were identified. Interviews with heads of all twenty organizations were pursued. Eleven were granted.

NOTES

PREFACE

1. This is a respondent from the Religious Leadership and Diversity Project. See Edwards 2019.

INTRODUCTION

1. Manning Marable's (1984) analysis of Jesse Jackson's candidacy for president suggests that it was a turning point in how black religious leaders and churches framed and participated in social action.
2. For example, Gaines (2010) proposes that black churches encourage their congregations to get actively involved in the local schools and education boards.
3. Religion is historically an integral part of mobilization and social change. See Stamatov 2011.

CHAPTER 1. ON THE FRONT LINES

1. I did see two other people in the parking lot that day who were not with the Democrats or OFA. One was an antiabortion protestor. Another parked his truck with Republican and sociopolitically right propaganda posted all over the vehicle.
2. I do not name this denomination in an effort to help protect the organization's and its leaders' identities. With an understanding of our study, I was invited to this denominational meeting. The COGIC data were public, and so we do name this organization.
3. Little Edwards contacted the people who sang the song. They informed her that the lyrics were written by Rev. Beverly A. Cofield and Rev. Eugene Schoolfield.
4. The singers were from the choir of a church of one the pastors who participated in this study, one who had the chance to meet President Obama on two separate occasions.
5. There are several more recent studies that call into question the importance of political processes, finding the role of political opportunity structures to be limited. See, for example, Banaszak 1996; McCammon 2001; Ganz 2009.
6. These phenomena have targeted poor urban blacks.
7. Matthew Desmond (2016) similarly highlights the parallel structures that severely disadvantage poor black people, claiming that where incarceration has defined the lives of poor black men, eviction has defined the lives of poor black women.
8. Ohio Republicans are continuing to propose laws that restrict voting. See Zuckerman 2021; Smyth 2021.
9. US Supreme Court did uphold a "Use it or Lose it" law in Ohio, spearheaded by Jon Husted, that allows the state to purge voter registrations not frequently used over most recent federal elections. See Williams 2018; Zuckerman 2021; ACLU Ohio 2012.

CHAPTER 2. THE OBAMA EFFECT

1. See Edwards 2016, which discusses how this issue is negotiated by black religious leaders.

CHAPTER 3. THE CIVIL RIGHTS MOVEMENT CREDENTIAL

1. Proponents of the political process theory suggest as much, arguing that activists choose to mobilize when there are advantageous political contexts in place (Meyer and Minkoff 2004). Where we add to political process theory is that we argue that the decision to act does not rest with activists or leaders broadly construed but with particular leaders, the principal leader.
2. Joel Andreas (2007) in his study of the Chinese cultural revolution also highlights the importance of charisma for movement leaders.
3. Jan Stutje (2012) highlights the role of charisma for leadership.
4. This work on charisma stems from social psychology. For a sociological perspective on charisma, see, for example, Friedland 1964; and Blau 1963.

CHAPTER 4. THE BLACK PROTESTANT ETHIC

1. This perspective does not fully account for why there is such residential turnaround among certain populations. Matthew Desmond's (2016) study of eviction shows that the relatively frequent residential mobility of blacks has more to do with the intersection of racist and sexist systems that severely disadvantage black mothers in the housing market, not irresponsibility and an unwarranted penchant for moving from place to place. Barbara Ehrenreich (2001) makes a similar argument about the working poor in *Nickel and Dimed: On Not Getting By in America*.
2. Critical whiteness theory argues that the foundation of racial hierarchies is whiteness, the taken-for-granted normativity of the culture of Anglos and their disproportionate location in positions of power. For more on this, see Doane and Bonilla-Silva 2003.
3. Barbara Reskin (2012) discusses how the racial discrimination system is best dismantled by unearthing the base causes of a system, not superficial causes.

CHAPTER 5. A DIFFERENT BALLGAME

1. Sharon Collins, in *Black Corporate Executives: The Making and Breaking of a Black Middle Class* (1996), addresses how this process also happens in the business world for upwardly mobile black managers.
2. There is a long-standing community organization that was at one point affiliated with the Gamaliel network called NOAH (Northeast Ohio Alliance for Hope) based in East Cleveland; this is a separate municipality from Cleveland. That organization used to cover more of the greater Cleveland metropolitan area (see Kleidman 2004), but at the time of this research, NOAH was focused on East Cleveland.

3. In fall 2017, the second author attended a candidate forum sponsored by the Amos Project at Brian McCormick's church. He was also one of the spokespeople for the organization's ultimately successful campaign to fund universal preschool in Cincinnati in 2016. While we do not have his perspective on his current involvement in Amos, his relationship with the organization has evolved over time.
4. This pattern persists in multiracial churches. See, for example, Christerson, Edwards, and Emerson 2005; Edwards 2008; and Barron 2016.

CHAPTER 6. THE GENERAL, THE WARRIOR, AND THE PROTÉGÉ

1. For more on brokers and their capacity to act as bridges for resource distribution, see Burt 2004. People who act as brokers also gain considerable cultural capital that can be used to elevate their status to leader within a network. For examples, see Padgett and Ansell 1993; Diani 2003; Lindsey 2008; and Stovel and Shaw 2012.
2. Wood and Fulton (2015) discuss in detail the potential of this approach. However, this is not an easy task. The percentage of black churches that were affiliated with FBCOs dropped precipitously over the first decade of this century. See Wood and Fulton 2015, 75–76.

CONCLUSION

1. Save a couple tepid supporters. One was less supportive because he was a bigger supporter of Hillary Clinton. Another was not supportive because of Obama's support of same-sex marriage.
2. Jack Goldstone (2004) argues that contemporary mobilization is more often than not led by political actors within democratic politics in an effort to influence politics rather than by the disadvantaged mobilizing for power. One could extend this idea to argue that black religious leaders are more a part of the democratic field vying for influence in politics rather than for justice and opportunity for blacks.
3. Over the years, FBCOs and national networks have implemented some changes to Alinsky's "rules" and techniques to address the political realities they face. Within the FBCO field, these methodological changes and variation between groups are the source of much discussion and conflict (Hall and Hall 1996). However, even given these changes and tactical diversity within the field, the broad contours of mobilization in FBCOs still follow the Alinsky blueprint in the ways we describe here.
4. I am grateful to Angela Davis, who during a university-sponsored speech that I attended several years ago reminded the audience of this fact.
5. For a discussion on the role of women in the civil rights movement, for example, see Morris 1984; Robnett 1997; and Herda-Rapp 1998.

REFERENCES

Abram, Dominic, and Michael Hogg. 1990. "Social Identification, Self-Categorization and Social Influence." *European Review of Social Psychology* 1:195–228.

ACLU Ohio. N.d. "Voting Rights." Accessed February 13, 2019. www.acluohio.org.

———.2012. "Secretary Husted Should Give Up the Ghost on Early Voting Restrictions." October 10, 2012. www.acluohio.org.

Alexander, Michelle. 2010. *The New Jim Crow: Mass Incarceration in the Age of Colorblindness*. New York: New Press.

Alinsky, Saul D. 1941. "Community Analysis and Organization." *American Journal of Sociology* 46:797–808.

Andreas, Joel. 2007. "The Structure of Charismatic Mobilization: A Case Study of Rebellion During the Chinese Cultural Revolution." *American Sociological Review* 72:434–58.

Andrews, Kenneth T. 2007. "Social Movements and Policy Implementations: The Mississippi Civil Rights Movement and the War on Poverty, 1965–1971." *American Sociological Review* 66:71–95.

Andrews, Kenneth T., Marshall Ganz, Matthew Baggetta, Hahrie Han, and Chaeyoon Lim. 2010. "Leadership, Membership and Voice: Civic Associations That Work." *American Journal of Sociology* 115:1191–1242.

Arkin, Daniel. 2015. "Donald Trump Criticized after He Appears to Mock Reporter Serge Kovaleski." *NBC News*, November 26, 2015. www.nbcnews.com.

Baer, Hans, and Merrill Singer. 1992. *African-American Religion in the Twentieth Century: Varieties of Protest and Accommodation*. Knoxville: University of Tennessee Press.

Baggetta, Matthew, Hahrie Han, and Kenneth T. Andrews. 2013. "Leading Associations: How Individual Characteristics and Team Dynamics Generate Committed Leaders." *American Sociological Review* 78:544–73.

Balmer, Randall. 2014. "The Real Origins of the Religious Right." *Politico*, May 27, 2014.

Balz, Dan. 2010. "The GOP Takeover in the States." *Washington Post*, November 13, 2010. www.washingtonpost.com.

Bamworth, Emily. 2017. "4 Churches and Synagogues Leave Greater Cleveland Congregations over Q Transformation Protests." *Cleveland.com*, July 7, 2017. http://cleveland.com.

Banaszak, Lee Ann. 1996. *Why Movements Succeed or Fail: Opportunity, Culture, and the Struggle for Woman Suffrage*. Princeton, NJ: Princeton University Press.

Banks, Adelle M. 2020. "After Getting Out the Vote, Black Church Leaders Look Ahead." *Christian Century*, December 14, 2020. www.christiancentury.org.

Barker, Colin, Alan Johnson, and Michael Lavalette. 2001. *Leadership and Social Movements.* Manchester: Manchester University Press.

Barnes, Sandra L. 2004. "Priestly and Prophetic Influences on Black Church Social Services." *Social Problems* 51:202–21.

———. 2005. "Black Church Culture and Community Action." *Social Forces* 84:967–94.

Barnes, Sandra L., and Oluchi Nwosu. 2014. "Black Church Electoral and Protest Politics from 2002 to 2012: A Social Media Analysis of the Resistance Versus Accommodation Dialectic." *Journal of African American Studies* 18:209–35.

Barron, Jessica M. 2016. "Managed Diversity: Race, Place, and an Urban Church." *Sociology of Religion* 77:18–36.

Baumann, Roger. 2016. "Political Engagement Meets the Prosperity Gospel: African American Christian Zionism and Black Church Politics." *Sociology of Religion* 77:359–85.

Bell, Joyce M., and Douglas Hartmann. 2007. "Diversity in Everyday Discourse: The Cultural Ambiguities and Consequences of 'Happy Talk.'" *American Sociological Review* 72:895–914.

Benford, Robert D., and David A. Snow. 2000. "Framing Processes and Social Movements: An Overview and Assessment." *Annual Review of Sociology* 26:611–39.

Berenson, William M.; Kirk W. Elifson, and Tandy Tollerson. 1976. "Preachers in Politics: A Study of Political Activism among the Black Ministry." *Journal of Black Studies* 6:373–92.

Bernstein, Mary. 2005. "Identity Politics." *Annual Review of Sociology* 31:47–74.

Beyerlein, Kraig, and Mark Chaves. 2003. "The Political Activities of Religious Congregations in the United States." *Journal for the Scientific Study of Religion* 42:229–46.

Billingsley, Andrew. 1999. *Mighty Like a River: The Black Church and Social Reform.* New York: Oxford University Press.

Black Lives Matter. N.d. "Our Cofounders." Accessed June 18, 2020. https://blacklivesmatter.com.

Blake, Charles E., Sr. 2012 "Presiding Bishop Urges Voter Registration." Church of God in Christ. www.cogic.org.

Blau, Peter M. 1963. "Critical Remarks on Weber's Theory of Authority." *American Political Science Review* 57:305–16.

Bobo, Lawrence. 2017. "Racism in Trump's America: Reflections on Culture, Sociology, and the 2016 US Presidential Election." *British Journal of Sociology* 68:S85–S104.

Bobo, Lawrence, James R. Kluegel, and Ryan A. Smith. 1996. "Laissez-Faire Racism: The Crystallization of a Kinder, Gentler Anti-Black Ideology." In *Racial Attitudes in the 1990s: Continuity and Change,* edited by Steven A. Tuch and Jack K. Martin, 15–44. Westport, CT: Praeger.

Bonilla-Silva, Eduardo. 2001. *White Supremacy and Racism in the Post-Civil Rights Era.* Boulder, CO: Lynne Reiner.

———. 2003. *Racism without Racists.* Lanham, MD: Rowman and Littlefield.

Bonilla-Silva, Eduardo, and Tyrone Forman. 2000. "'I Am Not a Racist but . . .': Mapping White College Students' Racial Ideology in the USA." *Discourse & Society* 11:50–85.

Bonilla-Silva, Eduardo, Amanda Lewis, and David G. Embrick. 2004. "'I Did Not Get That Job Because of a Black Man . . .': The Story Lines and Testimonies of Color-Blind Racism." *Sociological Forum* 19:555–81.

Brown, R. Khari. 2006. "Racial Differences in Congregation-Based Political Activism." *Social Forces* 84:1581–1604.

Brown, R. Khari, and Ronald E. Brown. 2003. "Faith and Works: Church-Based Social Capital Resources and African American Political Activism." *Social Forces* 82:617–41.

Burt, Ronald. 2004. "Structural Holes and Good Ideas." *American Journal of Sociology* 110:349–99.

Cavendish, James. 2003. "Church-Based Community Activism: A Comparison of Black and White Catholic Congregations." *Journal for the Scientific Study of Religion* 39:371–84.

Chaves, Mark, and Lynn Higgins. 1992. "Comparing the Community Involvement of Black and White Congregations." *Journal for the Scientific Study of Religion* 31:425–40.

Christerson, Brad, Korie L. Edwards, and Michael O. Emerson. 2005. *Against All Odds: The Struggle for Racial Integration in Religious Organizations.* New York: New York University Press.

Collins, Patricia Hill. 1986. "Learning from the Outsider-Within: The Sociological Significance of Black Feminist Thought." *Social Problems* 33:S14–S32.

———. 2006. "Some Group Matters: Intersectionality, Situated Standpoints, and Black Feminist Thought." In *Companion to African American Philosophy*, edited by T. L. Lott and J. P. Pittman, 205–29. Chichester, UK: Wiley-Blackwell.

Collins, Sharon M. 1996. *Black Corporate Executives: The Making and Breaking of a Black Middle Class.* Philadelphia: Temple University Press.

Cook, Elizabeth Adell, and Clyde Wilcox. 1990. "Religious Orientations & Political Attitudes among Blacks in Washington, DC." *Polity* 22:527–43.

Crawford, Sue E. S., and Laura R. Olson, eds. 2001. *Christian Clergy in American Politics.* Baltimore: Johns Hopkins University Press.

Cress, Daniel M., and David A. Snow. 1996. "Mobilization at the Margins: Resources, Benefactors and the Viability of Homeless Social Movement Organizations." *American Sociological Review* 61:1089–1109.

———. 2000. "The Outcomes of Homeless Mobilization: The Influence of Organization, Disruption, Political Mediation and Framing." *American Journal of Sociology* 105:1063–1104.

Denton, Robert E. 2005. "Religion and the 2004 Presidential Campaign." *American Behavioral Scientist* 49:11–31.

Desmond, Matthew. 2016. *Evicted: Poverty and Profit in the American City.* New York: Crown.

Diani, Mario. 2003. "'Leaders' or Brokers? Positions and Influence in Social Movement Networks." In *Social Movements and Networks: Relational Approaches to Collective Action*, edited by M. Diani and D. McAdam, 281–98. Oxford: Oxford University Press.

Djupe, Paul A., and Christopher P. Gilbert. 2002. "The Political Voice of Clergy." *Journal of Politics* 64:596–609.

DLVideos100. 2012. "Rev. Dr. William Barber, II Addresses the NAACP, July 11, 2012." YouTube, July 12, 2012. www.youtube.com.

Doane, Woody, and Eduardo Bonilla-Silva. 2003. *White Out: The Continuing Significance of Racism.* New York: Routledge.

Dovidio, John F., and Samuel Gaertner. 2004. "Aversive Racism." In *Advances in Experimental Social Psychology,* vol. 36, edited by M. P. Zanna, 1–52. San Diego, CA: Elsevier Academic Press, 2004. doi.org/10.1016/S0065-2601(04)36001-6.

DPA and Reuters. 2020. "Thousands March in Black Lives Matter Protests across Asia, from Australia to Japan." *South China Morning Post,* June 6, 2020. www.scmp.com.

DuBois, William Edward Burghardt. (1903) 2003. *The Negro Church.* New York: Rowman and Littlefield.

———. (1903) 2008. *The Souls of Black Folk.* New York: Bantam Classic.

Edwards, Korie L. 2008. *The Elusive Dream: The Power of Race in Interracial Churches.* New York: Oxford University Press.

———. 2016. "The Space Between: Exploring How Religious Leaders Reconcile Religion and Politics." *Journal for the Scientific Study of Religion* 55:271–87.

———. 2019. "Deconstructing a Research Journey: Methods and Lessons of the Religious Leadership and Diversity Project." *Sociology of Religion: A Quarterly Review* 80:415–34.

Edwards, Korie L., Brad Christerson, and Michael O. Emerson. 2013. "Race, Religious Organizations, and Integration." *Annual Review of Sociology* 39:211–28.

Edwards, Korie L., and Rebecca Kim. 2019. "Estranged Pioneers: The Case of African American and Asian American Multiracial Church Pastors." *Sociology of Religion* 80:456–77.

Ehrenreich, Barbara. 2001. *Nickel and Dimed: On (Not) Getting By in America.* New York: Holt.

Emerson, Michael O., and Christian Smith. 2000. *Divided by Faith: Evangelical Religion and the Problem of Race in America.* Oxford: Oxford University Press.

Fair Fight. 2020. Home page. December 12, 2020. https://fairfight.com/.

Fanon, Frantz. 1967. *Black Skin White Masks.* New York: Grove.

Fernandez, Roberto, and Doug McAdam. 1988. "Social Networks and Social Movements: Multiorganizational Fields and Recruitment to Mississippi Freedom Summer." *Sociological Forum* 3:357–82.

Fitzgerald, Scott T., and Ryan E. Spohn. 2005. "Pulpits and Platforms: The Role of the Church in Determining Protest among Black Americans." *Social Forces* 84:1015–48.

Frazier, E. Franklin. 1974. *The Negro Church in America.* New York: Schocken Books.

Friedland, William H. 1964. "For a Sociological Concept of Charisma." *Social Forces* 43:18–26.

Friedman, Debra, and Doug McAdam. 1992. "Collective Identity and Activism: Networks, Choices, and the Life of a Social Movement." In *Frontiers in Social Movement Theory,* edited by A. Morris and C. M. Mueller, 156–73. New Haven, CT: Yale University Press.

Gaines, Robert W. 2010. "Looking Back, Moving Forward: How the Civil Rights Era Church Can Guide the Modern Black Church in Improving Black Student Achievement." *Journal of Negro Education* 79 (3): 366–79.

Gallagher, Charles A. 2003. "Color-Blind Privilege: The Social and Political Functions of Erasing the Color Line in Post Race America." *Race, Gender & Class* 10:22–37.

Ganz, Marshall. 2000. "Resources and Resourcefulness: Strategic Capacity in the Unionization of California Agriculture, 1959–1966." *American Journal of Sociology* 105:1003–62.

———. 2009. *Why David Sometimes Wins: Leadership, Organization and Strategy in the California Farm Worker Movement*. Oxford: Oxford University Press.

———. 2010. "Leading Change: Leadership, Organization, and Social Movements." In *Handbook of Leadership Theory and Practice: A Harvard Business School Centennial Colloquium*, edited by Nitin Nohria and Rakesh Khurana, 527–68. Boston: Harvard Business Press. www.researchgate.net.

Gilkes, Cheryl T. 1998. "'Plenty Good Room': Adaptation in a Changing Black Church." *Annals of the American Academy of Political and Social Science* 558:101–21.

Glaude, Eddie, Jr. 2012. "The Black Church Is Dead." *HuffPost*, August 23, 2012. www.huffpost.com.

Goldstone, Jack A. 2004. "More Social Movements or Fewer? Beyond Political Opportunity Structures to Relational Fields." *Theory and Society* 3:3333–65.

Gomez, Henry J. 2019. "Obama Campaign Sues Ohio Secretary of State Jon Husted over Early Voting Restrictions." *Cleveland.com*, January 12. 2019. www.cleveland.com.

Gorski, Philip. 2017. "Why Evangelicals Voted for Trump: A Critical Cultural Sociology." *American Journal of Cultural Sociology* 5:338–54.

Graham, David A., Adrienne Green, Cullen Murphy, and Parker Richards. 2019. "An Oral History of Trump's Bigotry." *Atlantic*, June 2019. www.theatlantic.com.

Guth, James L., Linda Beail, Greag Crow, Beverly Gaddy, Steve Montreal, Breant Nelsen, James Penning, and Jeff Walz. 2003. "The Political Activity of Evangelical Clergy in the Election of 2000: A Case Study of Five Denominations." *Journal for the Scientific Study of Religion* 42:501–14.

Guth, James L., and J. C. Green, Corwin E. Smidt, L. A. Kellstedt, M. M. Poloma. 1997. *The Bully Pulpit: The Politics of Protestant Clergy*. Lawrence: University Press of Kansas.

Hall, Leda McIntyre, and Melvin F. Hall. 1996. "Big Fights: Competition Between Poor People's Social Movement Organizations." *Nonprofit and Voluntary Sector Quarterly* 25:53–72.

Han, Hahrie. 2014. *How Organizations Develop Activists: Civic Associations and Leadership in the 21st Century*. Oxford: Oxford University Press.

Harding, Sandra. 1993. "Rethinking Standpoint Epistemology: What Is Strong Objectivity?" In *Feminist Epistemologies*, edited by Linda Alcoff and Elizabeth Potter, 49–82. New York: Routledge.

Harris, Fredrick C. 1994. "Something Within: Religion as a Mobilizer of African-American Political Activism." *Journal of Politics* 56:42–68.

———. 1999. *Something Within: Religion and African American Political Activism*. New York: Oxford University Press.

Hart, Gabby. 2020. "Black Lives Matter Protests Mark Historic Civil Rights Movement, UNLV Professor Says." *3News*, June 11, 2020. https://news3lv.com.

Hartsock, Nancy. 1983. "The Feminist Standpoint: Developing the Ground for a Specifically Feminist Historical Materialism." In *Discovering Reality: Feminist Perspectives on Epistemology, Metaphysics, Methodology, and Philosophy of Science*, edited by Sandra Harding and Merrill B. Hintikka, 283–310. Amsterdam: Kluwer Academic.

Haslam, S. Alexander, and Michael J. Platow. 2001. "The Link between Leadership and Followership: How Affirming Social Identity Translates Vision into Action." *Personality and Social Psychology Bulletin* 27:1469–79.

Herda-Rapp, Ann. 1998. "The Power of Informal Leadership: Women Leaders in the Civil Rights Movement." *Sociological Focus* 31:341–55.

Higginbotham, Evelyn Brooks. 1993. *Righteous Discontent: The Women's Movement in the Black Baptist Church, 1880–1920*. Cambridge, MA: Harvard University Press.

Hogg, Michael A. 2001. "A Social Identity Theory of Leadership." *Personality and Social Psychology Review* 5:184–200.

Hogg, Michael A., and Daan van Knippenberg. 2003. "Social Identity and Leadership Processes in Groups." In *Advances in Experimental Social Psychology*, vol. 35, edited by M. P. Zanna, 1–52. San Diego, CA: Elsevier Academic Press. doi.org/10.1016/S0065-2601(03)01001-3.

Hogg, Michael A., and John C. Turner. 1987. "Intergroup Behaviour, Self-Stereotyping and the Salience of Social Categories." *British Journal of Social Psychology* 26:325–40.

Hughey, Matthew. 2012. *White Bound: Nationalists, Antiracists, and the Shared Meanings of Race*. Stanford, CA: Stanford University Press.

Hunt, Scott, and Robert Benford. 2004. "Collective Identity, Solidarity, and Commitment." In *The Blackwell Companion to Social Movements*, edited by D. Snow, S. Soule, and H. Kriesi, 433–57. Malden, MA: Blackwell.

Jenkins, Craig. 1983. "Resource Mobilization Theory and the Study of Social Movements." *Annual Review of Sociology* 9:527–53.

Johnson, Eric. 2012. "The Keys to Winning in Swing State Ohio in Presidential Race." *Reuters*, November 5, 2012. www.reuters.com.

Jones, Jeffrey M. 2011. "Obama Approval Slips among Blacks, Hispanics in March." Gallup, April 7, 2011. www.gallup.com.

Kinder, Donald R., and David O. Sears. 1981. "Prejudice and Politics: Symbolic Racism versus Racial Threats to the Good Life." *Journal of Personality and Social Psychology* 40:414–31.

Kitschelt, Herbert. 1986. "Political Opportunity Structure and Political Protest: Anti-Nuclear Movements in Four Democracies." *British Journal of Political Science* 16:57–85.

Klandermans, Bert, and Dirk Oegema. 1987. "Potentials, Networks, Motivations, and Barriers: Steps Towards Participation in Social Movements." *American Sociological Review* 52:519–31.

Kleidman, Robert. 2004. "Community Organizing and Regionalism." *City and Community* 3 (4): 403–21.

Knippenberg, Dan van. 2011. "Embodying Who We Are: Leader Group Prototypicality and Leadership Effectiveness." *Leadership Quarterly* 22:1078–91.

Knippenberg, Dan van, and Michael Hogg. 2001. "Social Identity Processes in Organizations." *Group Processes and Intergroup Relations* 4:185–89.

Knippenberg, Dan van, Nathalie Lossie, and Henk Wilkie. 1994. "In-Group Prototypicality and Persuasion: Determinants of Heuristic and Systematic Message Processing." *British Journal of Social Psychology* 33:289–300.

Lee, Shayne. 2003. "The Church of Faith and Freedom: Black Baptists and Social Change." *Journal for the Scientific Study of Religion* 42:31–34.

Lee, Trymaine. 2012. "Ohio Early Voting Ruling Appealed by John Husted, Deepening Confusion over Election Laws." *HuffPost*, October 11, 2012. www.huffingtonpost.com.

Lincoln, C. Eric, and Lawrence H. Mamiya. 1990. *The Black Church in the African American Experience*. Durham, NC: Duke University Press.

Lindsay, D. Michael. 2008. "Evangelicals in the Power Elite: Elite Cohesion Advancing a Movement." *American Sociological Review* 73:60–82.

Lipka, Michael, and Gregory A. Smith. 2020. "White Evangelical Approval of Trump Slips, but Eight-in-Ten Say They Would Vote for Him." Pew Research Center, July 1, 2020. www.pewresearch.org.

Liubchenkova, Natalie. 2020. "In Pictures: Black Lives Matter Protests Taking on the World." *Euronews*, June 15, 2020. www.euronews.com.

Lord, Robert G., Douglas J. Brown, and Jennifer L. Harvey. 2001. "System Constraints on Leadership Perceptions, Behavior and Influence: An Example of Connectionist Level Processes." In *Blackwell Handbook of Social Psychology: Group Processes*, edited by M. A. Hogg and S. Tindale, 283–310. Oxford, UK: Blackwell.

Marable, Manning. 1984. "The Rainbow Coalition: Jesse Jackson and the Politics of Ethnicity." *CrossCurrents* 34:21–42.

Martin, Andrew. 2007. "Organizational Structure, Authority, and Protest: The Case of Union Organizing in the United States, 1990–2001." *Social Forces* 85:1413–35.

———. 2008. "Resources for Success: Social Movements, Strategic Resource Allocation and Union Organizing Outcomes." *Social Problems* 55:501–24.

Martin, Jonathan. 2012. "2012: The Battle for 7 States." *Politico*, October 23, 2012. www.politico.com.

Martinez, Jessica, and Gregory A. Smith. 2016. "How the Faithful Voted: A Preliminary 2016 Analysis." Pew Research Center, November 9, 2016. www.pewresearch.org.

Mays, Benjamin Elijah, and Joseph William Nicholson. 1933. *The Negro's Church*. New York: Aron.

McAdam, Doug. 1982. *Political Process and the Development of Black Insurgency 1930–1970*. Chicago: University of Chicago Press.

———. 1986. "Recruitment to High-Risk Activism: The Case of Freedom Summer." *American Journal of Sociology* 92:64–90.

McCammon, Holly. 2001. "Stirring Up Suffrage Sentiment: The Formation of the State Woman Suffrage Organizations." *Social Forces* 85:449–80.

McCarthy, John D., and Mark Wolfson. 1996. "Resource Mobilization by Local Social Movement Organizations: Agency, Strategy and Organization in the Movement against Drinking and Driving." *American Sociological Review* 61:1070–88.

McCarthy, John D., and Mayer N. Zald. 1977. "Resource Mobilization Theory and Social Movements: A Partial Theory." *American Journal of Sociology* 82:1212–41.

———. 2002. "The Enduring Vitality of the Resource Mobilization Theory of Social Movements." In *Handbook of Sociological Theory*, edited by J. Turner, 533–65. New York: Kluwer Academic / Plenum.

McDaniel, Eric L. 2003. "Black Clergy in the 2000 Election." *Journal for the Scientific Study of Religion* 42:533–46.

———. 2008. *Politics in the Pews: The Political Mobilization of Black Churches*. Ann Arbor: University of Michigan Press.

McRoberts, Omar. 2003. *Streets of Glory: Church and Community in a Black Urban Neighborhood*. Chicago: University of Chicago Press.

Meyer, David, and Debra Minkoff. 2004. "Conceptualizing Political Opportunity." *Social Forces* 82:1457–92.

Morris, Aldon. 1981. "Black Southern Student Sit-In Movement: An Analysis of Internal Organization." *American Sociological Review* 46:755–67.

———. 1984. *The Origins of the Civil Rights Movement: Black Communities Organizing for Change*. New York: Free Press.

———. 2000. "Reflections on Social Movement Theory: Criticisms and Proposals." *Contemporary Sociology* 29:445–54.

Morris, Aldon, and Cedric Herring. 1984. "Theory and Research in Social Movements: A Critical Review." Prepublication manuscript. Deep Blue Repositories, University of Michigan Library.

Morris, Aldon, and Suzanne Staggenborg. 2007. "Leadership in Social Movements." In *The Blackwell Companion to Social Movements*, edited by D. A. Snow, S. Soule, and H. Kriesi, 171–96. Oxford, UK: Blackwell.

Munn, Christopher W. 2019. "Finding a Seat at the Table: How Race Shapes Access to Social Capital." *Sociology of Religion* 80:435–55.

Nagel, Joane. 1994. "Constructing Ethnicity: Creating and Recreating Ethnic Identity and Culture." *Social Problems* 41:152–76.

Neal, Samantha. 2017. "Views of Racism as a Major Problem Increase Sharply, Especially among Democrats." Pew Research Center, August 29, 2017. www.pewresearch.org.

Ohio Legislature. N.d. "Ohio Revised Code: Section 3501.30: Polling Place Supplies." Accessed August 26, 2015. http://codes.ohio.gov.

Olson, Laura. 2000. *Filled with Spirit and Power: Protestant Clergy in Politics*. Albany: State University of New York Press.

Omi, Michael, and Howard Winant. 1994. *Racial Formation in the United States: From the 1960s to the 1990s*. 2nd ed. New York: Routledge.

Oyakawa, Michelle. 2017. "Building a Movement in the Non-Profit Industrial Complex." PhD diss., Ohio State University.

Padgett, John F., and Christopher K. Ansell. 1993. "Robust Action and the Rise of the Medici, 1400–1434." *American Journal of Sociology* 98:1259–1319.

Page, Susan, and Paul Overberg. 2013. "A Changing America: In 2012, Blacks Outvoted Whites." *USA Today*, May 8, 2013. www.usatoday.com.

Pattillo-McCoy, Mary. 1998. "Church Culture as a Strategy of Action in the Black Community." *American Sociological Review* 63:767–84.

Perry, Samuel L. 2012. "Diversity, Donations, and Disadvantage: The Implications of Personal Fundraising for Racial Diversity in Evangelical Outreach Ministries." *Review of Religious Research* 53:397–418.

Pew Research Center. 2017. *In America, Does More Education Equal Less Religion?* Washington, DC: Pew Research Center.

Phillips, Steve. 2016. *Brown Is the New White: How a Demographic Revolution Has Created a New American Majority*. New York: New Press.

Pico Network. N.d. "History." Accessed November 27, 2013. www.piconetwork.org.

Pinn, Anthony B. 2002. *Black Church in the Post-Civil Rights Era*. Maryknoll, NY: Orbis Books.

Polletta, Francesca, and James Jasper. 2001. "Collective Identity and Social Movements." *Annual Review of Sociology* 27:283–305.

PRRI. 2016. "Backing Trump, White Evangelicals Flip Flop on Importance of Candidate Character." October 19, 2016. www.prri.org.

Putnam, Robert, and David Campbell. 2010. *American Grace: How Religion Unites and Divides Us*. New York: Simon and Schuster.

Ray, Rashawn. 2020. "How Black Americans Saved Biden and American Democracy." Brookings Institution, November 24, 2020. www.brookings.edu.

Reese, Laura, Ronald Brown, and James David Ivers. 2007. "'Some Children See Him . . .': Political Participation and the Black Christ." *Political Behavior* 29:517–37.

Reskin, Barbara. 2012. "The Race Discrimination System." *Annual Review of Sociology* 38:17–35.

Rice, Rachel. 2020. "Black Men Put On Suits and Ties to March against Oppression in St. Louis, Protests Continue in Florissant." *St. Louis Post-Dispatch*, June 8, 2020. www.stltoday.com.

Robnett, Belinda. 1997. *How Long? How Long? African-American Women in the Struggle for Civil Rights*. New York: Oxford University Press.

Rochefort, David, and Roger Cobb. 1993. "Problem Definition, Agenda Access and Policy Choice." *Policy Studies Journal* 21:56–71.

Ryan, Barbara. 2001. *Identity Politics in the Women's Movement*. New York: New York University Press.

Sam, Joseph. 2020. "City of Grace Church Plans Gathering of Black Male Excellence." *Fox28* (Columbus), June 7, 2020. https://myfox28columbus.com.

Shelton, Jason, and Michael O. Emerson. 2012. *Blacks and Whites in Christian America: How Racial Discrimination Shapes Religious Convictions.* New York: New York University Press.

Siegel, David A. 2009. "Social Networks and Collective Action." *American Journal of Political Science* 53:122–38.

Smidt, Corwin E. 2003. *Pulpit and Politics: Clergy in American Politics at the Advent of the Millennium.* Waco, TX: Baylor University Press.

Smith, David. 2012. "A Guide to the Must-Win States for Obama and Romney." *The Conversation*, October 29, 2012. https://theconversation.com.

Smith, Gregory A. 2005. "The Influence of Priests on the Political Attitudes of Roman." *Journal for the Scientific Study of Religion* 44:291–306.

Smyth, Julie Carr. 2021. "Ohio is Latest State to See GOP-Backed Voting Law Rewrite." *AP News*, May 6. 2021. www. apnews.com.

Snow, David A., and Robert Benford. 1988. "Ideology, Frame Resonance, and Participant Mobilization." *International Social Movement Research* 1:197–217.

Snow, David A., E. Burke Rochford, Steven Worden, and Robert Benford. 1986. "Frame Alignment Processes, Micromobilization, and Movement Participation." *American Sociological Review* 51:464–81.

Stamatov, Peter. 2011. "The Religious Field and the Path Dependent Transformation of Popular Politics in the Anglo American World, 1770–1840." *Theory and Society* 40:437–73.

Starkey, Jessi. 2020. "Community Hosts Demonstration of Black Excellence at Columbus City Hall." *abc6*, June 7, 2020. https://abc6onyourside.com.

Stovel, Katherine, and Lynette Shaw. 2012. "Brokerage." *Annual Review of Sociology* 38:139–58.

Stutje, Jan Willem. 2012. *Charismatic Leadership and Social Movements: The Revolutionary Power of Ordinary Men and Women.* New York: Berghahn.

Swidler, Ann. 1986. "Culture in Action: Symbols and Strategies." *American Sociological Review* 51:273–86.

Tarrow, Sidney. 1994. *Power In Movement: Social Movements, Collective Action, and Politics.* Cambridge: Cambridge University Press.

Tilly, Charles. 1978. *From Mobilization to Revolution.* Reading, MA: Addison-Wesley.

Tope, Daniel, Brittany D. Rawlinson, Justin T. Pickett, Amy Burdette, and Christopher Ellison. 2017. "Religion, Race, and Othering Barack Obama." *Social Currents* 4:51–70.

Turner, John C. 1991. *Social Influence.* Belmont, WA: Thomson Brooks / Cole.

Van Dyke, Nella. 2003. "Crossing Movement Boundaries: Factors That Facilitate Coalition Protest by American College Students, 1930–1990." *Social Problems* 50:226–250.

Van Dyke, Nella, and Sarah A. Soule. 2002. "Structural Social Change and the Mobilizing Effect of Threat: Explaining Levels of Patriot and Militia Organizing in the United States." *Social Problems* 49:497–520.

Verba, Sidney, Kay Lehman, and Henry Brady. 1995. *Voice and Equality: Civic Voluntarism in American Politics.* Cambridge, MA: Harvard University Press.

Wacquant, Loïc. 2014. "Class, Race and Hyperincarceration in Revanchist America." *Socialism and Democracy* 28:35–56.

Wald, Kenneth D. 1989. *Religion and Politics in the United States*. New York: Rowan and Littlefield.

Walsh, John. 2018. "11 Insults Trump Has Hurled at Women." *Business Insider*, October 17, 2018. www.businessinsider.com.

Warren, Mark. 2001. *Dry Bones Rattling: Community Building to Revitalize American Democracy*. Princeton, NJ: Princeton University Press.

Warren, Mark, and Richard L. Wood. 2001. *Faith-Based Community Organizing: The State of the Field*. Jericho, NY: Interfaith Funders.

Waxman, Olivia B. 2021. "Stacey Abrams and Other Georgia Organizers Are Part of a Long—But Often Overlooked—Tradition of Black Women Working for the Vote." *Time*, January 8, 2021. https://time.com.

Weber, Max. 1947. *The Theory of Social and Economic Organization*. Glencoe, NY: Free Press.

———. 1968. *Economy and Society*. Edited by Guenther Roth and Claus Wittich. New York: Bedminister.

Whitehead, Andrew, Samuel Perry, and Joseph Baker. 2018. "Make America Christian Again: Christian Nationalism and Voting for Donald Trump in the 2016 Presidential Election." *Sociology of Religion* 79:147–71.

Williams, Pete. 2018. "Supreme Court Gives Ohio Right to Purge Thousands of Voters from its Rolls. NBC News, June 11, 2018. www.nbcnews.com.

Wilson, William Julius. 1978. *The Declining Significance of Race: Blacks and Changing American Institutions*. Chicago: University of Chicago Press.

Wood, Richard L. 2002. *Faith in Action: Religion, Race, and Democratic Organizing in America*. Chicago: University of Chicago Press.

Wood, Richard L., and Brad R. Fulton. 2015. *A Shared Future: Faith-Based Organizing for Racial Equity and Ethical Democracy*. Chicago: University of Chicago Press.

Wood, Richard L., Brad R. Fulton, and Kathryn Partridge. 2012. *Building Bridges, Building Power: Developments in Institution-Based Community Organizing*. Longmont, CO: Interfaith Funders. www.soc.duke.edu.

Woodberry, Robert D., and Christian S. Smith. 1998. "Fundamentalism et al.: Conservative Protestants in America." *Annual Review of Sociology* 24:25–56.

Wuthnow, Robert. 1999. "Mobilizing Civic Engagement: The Changing Impact of Religious Involvement." In *Civic Engagement in American Democracy*, edited by T. Skocpol and M. P. Fiorina, 331–63. Washington, DC: Brookings Institute Press.

Zuckerman, Jake. 2021. "Ohio House Republicans Propose Voter Photo ID Law, Ending Most Absentee Voting." 10 WBNS, August 18, 2021. www.10tv.com.

INDEX

activists/activism, 6, 8, 21, 29, 60, 61, 62, 83, 121, 122, 132, 157, 162

African American(s), 3, 6, 30, 31, 73, 79, 81, 82, 83, 115, 116, 127, 130, 131, 149; activism, 8; Baptists, 149; black religious leaders and, 71; black religious leaders' views on, 77, 78, 79, 80, 120, 128; boys, 82; Christians, 30; church(es), 8, 29, 69, 81, 82, 104, 124; civic and political engagement, 8, 156; and civil rights movement, 6, 149; community, 82, 127, 131; and criminal justice system, 128; culture, 73; economic disadvantage, 81; and education, 78, 81, 128; and employment, 76, 128; faith, 68, 101, 103, 104; family, 78, 79, 82, 120; incarceration, 81, 128; inequality, 73; leaders, 6, 23, 131; men, 34, 75, 76, 82, 83; Obama, Barack, 34, 36, 38, 39; Obama for America, 4; in Ohio, 31, 124; and personal responsibility, 74–78; poverty, 124, 128; president, 36; and prison, 81; and racism and discrimination, 122; social welfare, 124; unarmed murders, 2; unemployment 124; voters, 17, 27, 30; and voting laws, 13, 156; women, vii, 2, 84, 85, 152, 153, 161, 163. See also blacks

African Methodist Episcopal denomination, 8

Afro-Citizens Unite, 116–117, 119, 122

Alexander, Michelle, 128

Alinsky model, 148, 149, 163

Alinsky, Saul, 148, 163n3 Conclusion. See also faith-based community organizing

Allen, Richard, 8, 111

Amos Project, 98–102, 106, 163

Arbery, Ahmaud, 2, 7

asset-based community development, 98, 120

Barber, William, II, 25

Belafonte, Harry, 118

Bethune, Mary McLeod, 111

Bible, vii, viii, 114

Biden, Joe, vii, 146

Birmingham, 126

black-centered civic organizations, 6, 87, 88, 89, 90, 93, 107, 108, 137, 157

black church, 4, 14, 91: and black community, vii, 86, 150; and civil rights movement, 2, 86, 152; culture, 8, 150, 156; and faith-based community organizing, 26, 91, 129, 134, 150; and gender, 84; Glaude, Eddie, Jr., on, 16; and mobilization, 9, 10, 67–68, 86, 134, 156; resources, 86, 156; theology, 83; and voter mobilization, 61; women, 84. See also African American(s): church(es)

black denominational alliance, 67–68

black feminist epistemology, 155

Black Lives Matter, 1, 2, 3, 4, 5, 7, 13, 92, 139, 146, 151, 153, 156

black minister (pastor or religious leader), vii, ix: and African American Baptists, 149; attitudes about black-white inequality, 71, 73–78, 83; attitudes about family, 78–82; attitudes about race, racism, 1, 5, 8, 38, 42–47, 50, 55, 77, 82, 137;

ABOUT THE AUTHORS

Korie Little Edwards is a leading scholar of race and religion in the United States and author of numerous articles and books on the subject, including *The Elusive Dream: The Power of Race in Interracial Churches*. Her work has been featured in several outlets including NPR, the *Columbus Dispatch*, the *Philadelphia Tribune*, the *Seattle Times*, and *Christianity Today*. She is also past president of the Society for the Scientific Study of Religion, an international, interdisciplinary association.

Michelle Oyakawa studies leaders and organizations that work for social change. She is coauthor of *Prisms of the People: Power and Organizing in Twenty-First Century America*, with Hahrie Han and Liz McKenna. Her dissertation about foundation funding of social movement organizations won the 2018 Outstanding Dissertation Award from the Collective Behavior and Social Movements Section of the American Sociological Association. She has published articles in several peer-reviewed journals, including *Sociology of Religion* and *Qualitative Sociology*.

Lightning Source UK Ltd.
Milton Keynes UK
UKHW012255040122
396612UK00003B/202